D1298139

On the Poetry of William Heyen . . .

On *Depth of Field* (1970):

"A brilliant first volume with a broad, coherent, and deeply moving design. . . . Suffice it to say that its author seems destined to be an important poet."
— John Irwin in *Poetry*

"It has great reserves of quiet. In the development of the modern lyric, it makes clear how much clearing and cleansing has been going on."
— Arthur Oberg in *The Southern Review*

"One of the more striking first collections of poems published this past year. . . . Heyen's poetry resembles Frost's in its fond and reverent concentration on nature, various aspects of which are captured in detailed, graphic descriptions. One is reminded of Frost's well-known dictum that a poem 'begins in delight and ends in wisdom' when reading Heyen's title poem and his 'Existential'" . . .
— Raymond Smith in *Modern Poetry Studies*

On *Noise in the Trees* (1974) and *Long Island Light* (1979):

"As Twain undeniably altered the Mississippi, as Thoreau forever changed Walden Pond, William Heyen has transformed Long Island. . . . A wonderful testament to the organic nature of artistic creation."
— Susan Astor

"He stands in the line of the Emersonian visionary. . . . He feels, too, the darkness of the American heart. . . . I think that if Robinson Jeffers read Heyen's poems he would find a poet of mature and simple eloquence, a poet whose music shaped the physical and psychological reality as many of us know it must be."
— Dave Smith in *American Poetry Review*

"Heyen is a wonderful poet. His Long Island is that kosmos where a gesture is a ceremony and a poem a blessing."
— Michael Waters

"Heyen's 'lifestudies' embrace history as well as man and his island, and find life rich and deep."
— Norman Holmes Pearson

"Authentic poems . . . steeped in remembrance of locale, . . . haunted by images of animals, Indians, going back to one's beginnings, the sources of joy."
— Daniel Hoffman in Philadelphia *Bulletin*

On *The Swastika Poems* (1977) and
  Erika: Poems of the Holocaust (1984):

"I lay the book down, heartsick, with a scream rising to my lips of the
horse dying in the Picasso painting, *Guernica*. I have written many
poems of the brutality of man to man, but not one has been able to
cleanse me of the blood of those crimes, and now *The Swastika Poems*.
What is there to say? I bow my head, sickened, until death takes me."
          — David Ignatow

"A surprisingly powerful work — surprising because we think of the
Nazi attempt to exterminate the Jews as a horror which has now
receded into a nightmare past. Heyen, because he is truly a poet, knows
better — knows that it is a horror which will renew itself over and over
as long as human beings ask the inescapable question: *What is man?* For
it is this question which haunts these poems. Heyen is himself an
American. But he is an American who is the son of a German of the
generation which produced the Nazis and the nephew of a Nazi flyer
shot down over Russia, and the question, *What is man?*, becomes for
him the more agonizing question, *What am I?* This question only poetry
can answer — and poetry only when it is written with discipline and
honesty and courage and restraint. As this book is written."
          — Archibald MacLeish

"There are events in our time we dare not look away from, but which
only an artist can make transfiguring sense from. This is what *The
Swastika Poems* do."
          — William Meredith

"Much more than a fine collection of poems and prose pieces; it is a
major human document whose cumulative impact gathers up and
transcends even the finest of its individual lyrics."
          — *Choice*

"The most powerful book I have read this year is William Heyen's *The
Swastika Poems*. . . . I know no other book so firmly integrated. . . .
Sober and chilling, songs in shadowed measures, each leading forward
into intenser realizations, darker clarities, these poems will invade
your dreams."
          — Hayden Carruth in *The Nation*

"For me, after two years of interviews with former Nazi doctors and
Auschwitz survivors, *The Swastika Poems* was healing in a way I found
nothing less than exhilarating, . . . and I have not had a similar sense
of artistic transcendence since the film *Night and Fog.* "
          — Robert Jay Lifton

[*The Swastika Poems* is] "perhaps the best book of poems by an Ameri-
can poet in this decade. It will be remembered long after more popular,
undeservedly praised books have been long forgotten."
          — Martin Grossman in *Skywriting*

"This is the poet with the 'right credentials.' And this is where the true holocaust poems come from. I doubt if they can be equalled."
— Karl Shapiro

[*Erika* is] "an act of strenuous self witness, . . . about the function of the imagination — its power and its limits when it comes up against the presumably untransformable facts of the Holocaust . . . as in the incredibly powerful "Poem Touching the Gestapo" or "The Trains."
— Jorie Graham in *New York Times Book Review*

"The poems succeed because they manage completely to free themselves of the maudlin, the sentimental-cum-sensational guilt-horrors, the posturings, vanities and easy penitential gestures that the subject could invite. He has saved himself by arduous artistic integrity."
— Anthony Hecht

On *The City Parables* (1980):

"Some poets are makers of lines, some of single poems, and some, like William Heyen, have the stamina and resourcefulness to work in long suites or sequences. The poems of this new book . . . are laced together by theme and image and swept by one flow of feeling. *The City Parables* takes on some great fears and struggles free of them; it is a book of considerable cumulative force."
— Richard Wilbur

On *Lord Dragonfly: Five Sequences* (1981):

"The *Lord Dragonfly* sequence is startling. I know of no Westerner who has come closer to pure haiku spirit."
— Lucien Stryk

"Heyen may feel the failures of this secular, murderous century most grievously, . . . but he keeps the mystic vision alive, the spark of splendor."
— Michael McFee

On *The Chestnut Rain* (1986):

"Heyen has attempted ambitious books before. His *Long Island Light* (1979) was a unified work of obsession and return to the country of his youth; and *Erika* (1984) was an unforgettable human document on the Holocaust. But I think it is *The Chestnut Rain*, purportedly a dozen years in the writing, which will ensure Heyen's place among the poets of his time."
— Robert Phillips

"One of the most profound meditations in all of American poetry in the spiritual legacy Whitman hoped to pass on to us, Heyen's *The Chestnut Rain* is a rare, dear, and transforming experience. It is a turning towards the light, this extraordinary sequence by a master wordsmith, a long poem by turns elegiac, erotic, consoling, violent, but always caring. Here is the tender evocation of our lost world, a world remembered now only in sepia photos, the world of majestic chestnut trees which stood as symbols of our past, when we lived closer to the living roots of things. I read these pages and ask, how is it that — with our nightmare history to haunt us — we have been blessed with such a poem as this?"
— Paul Mariani

"*The Chestnut Rain* is a surprising, beautiful 52-part epic on the plight of the American farmer, America's wars (especially Vietnam) and so much more. If you restrict yourself to one poetry collection this year, let this be it."
— George Myers, Jr. in *Columbus Dispatch*

On *Brockport, New York: Beginning with "And"* (1988):

"Among poets who have staked out particular communities as their literary domains, William Heyen is among the most fluent and musical. . . . While he cannot exclude the raging larger world, he upholds his community as the source of personal security and solace. . . . The beauties of Heyen's verse magnify its modesty."
— *Booklist*

On *Falling from Heaven: Holocaust Poems of a Jew and a Gentile* (1991):

"*Falling from Heaven* is a painful and poignant offering which reminds me that none of us has survived the Holocaust without scars. Yet, the distinguished work of the poets gives us the hope that maybe, if we are careful and courageous and alert and loving, maybe we can avoid a recurrence of such horror."
— Maya Angelou

On *Pterodactyl Rose: Poems of Ecology* (1991):

". . . a poetry of scrupulous attention, of love, of rich memory, of hope quickened and braced by the imagination. It is a poetry that remembers, and imagines, loss, in order to point a way of recovery."
— Jarold Ramsey

"These are strong poems. Sometimes the sadness in them is nearly debilitating. But sadness may lead to anger and hence to action. At any rate they are true, as potent as the latest scientific bulletin."
— Bill McKibben

THE HOST

SELECTED POEMS

1965 — 1990

Books by

WILLIAM HEYEN

Poetry

Depth of Field   (1970)
Noise in the Trees: Poems and a Memoir   (1974)
The Swastika Poems   (1977)
Long Island Light: Poems and a Memoir   (1979)
The City Parables   (1980)
Lord Dragonfly: Five Sequences   (1981)
Erika: Poems of the Holocaust   (1984) (1991)
The Chestnut Rain   (1986)
Brockport, New York: Beginning with "And"   (1988)
Falling from Heaven: Holocaust Poems of a Jew and a Gentile
(*with Louis Daniel Brodsky*)   (1991)
Pterodactyl Rose: Poems of Ecology   (1991)
Ribbons: The Gulf War — A Poem   (1991)

Anthologies

A Profile of Theodore Roethke   (1971)
American Poets in 1976   (1976)
The Generation of 2000: Contemporary American Poets   (1984)

Fiction

Vic Holyfield and the Class of 1957: A Romance   (1986)

THE HOST

SELECTED POEMS

1965 — 1990

WILLIAM HEYEN

TIME BEING BOOKS®
POETRY IN SIGHT AND SOUND

Time Being Books®
10411 Clayton Road
St. Louis, Missouri 63131

Time Being Books® is an imprint of Time Being Press, Inc.
St. Louis, Missouri

Time Being Books® volumes are printed on acid-free paper, and binding materials are chosen for strength and durability.

Library of Congress Cataloging-in-Publication Data

Heyen, William, 1940—
    [Poems. Selections]
    The host : selected poems, 1965—1990 / by William Heyen.
       p. cm.
    ISBN 1-877770-52-3 (HC) — ISBN 1-877770-53-1 (PB)
    I. Title.
    PS3558.E85A6   1994   93-33843
    811'.54—dc20   CIP

Cover design by Tony Tharenos
Book design and typesetting by Lori Loesche
Manufactured in the United States of America

First Edition, first printing (April 1994)

Acknowledgments

Books from which I've selected these poems written between 1965 and 1990 were first published as follows: *Depth of Field* (Baton Rouge: Louisiana State University Press, 1970); *Noise in the Trees* (New York: Vanguard Press, 1974); *The Swastika Poems* (New York: Vanguard Press, 1977); *Long Island Light* (New York: Vanguard Press, 1979); *The City Parables* (Athens, Ohio: Croissant & Co., 1980); *Lord Dragonfly: Five Sequences* (New York: Vanguard Press, 1981); *Erika* (New York: Vanguard Press, 1984); *The Chestnut Rain* (New York: Ballantine, 1986); *Brockport, New York: Beginning with "And"* (Dallas: Northouse & Northouse, 1988); *Falling from Heaven* (St. Louis: Time Being Books, 1991); and *Pterodactyl Rose* (St. Louis: Time Being Books, 1991). Grateful acknowledgment also to the editors of the many small presses that published limited edition broadsides and chapbooks of my poetry over twenty-five years: Abattoir Editions; Challenger Press; Metacom Press; Palaemon Press; Perishable Press; Rook Press; Scarab Press; The Sceptre Press (England); Sisyphus Editions; The Stone House Press; Tamarack Editions; and especially William B. Ewert, Publisher.

Periodicals in which poems in *The Host* first appeared include *American Poetry Review, The American Review, Ann Arbor Review, American Scholar, Avenue, Commentary, Crop Dust, Fireweed, The Georgia Review, Harper's, The Humanist, The Iowa Review, John Berryman Studies, Modern Poetry Studies, The New Yorker, New York Times, The Ohio Review, Ontario Review, Pembroke Magazine, Ploughshares, Poetry, Poetry Northwest, Prairie Schooner, The Southern Review, Sycamore, TriQuarterly, The University of Windsor Review, Upstate, Verse,* and *Virginia Quarterly Review.*

I'm indebted to SUNY College at Brockport for sabbaticals, and to the John Simon Guggenheim Memorial Foundation, National Endowment for the Arts, and New York State Foundation for the Arts for writing fellowships.

Wendell Berry and Donald Hall were kind enough to help me clarify some lines in the 38th section of *The Chestnut Rain*. Finally, thanks to Sheri Vandermolen of Time Being Books for her close reading of *The Host* in manuscript, and to Lori Loesche for her work with design and typesetting.

W.H.

For Han

The Eye

As I begin, not knowing what, to write,
the sun, from the clip on my pen,
turns on this page,

such a streaked, burst gold eye,

all I have, all I have ever wanted, you
to see this, to see with this,
in case it is dark where you live.

Contents

~ from ~

Erika *(1984)*

The Chestnut Rain *(1986)*

~ from ~

Brockport, New York:
Beginning with "And" *(1988)*

~ from ~

Falling from Heaven *(1991)*

~ from ~

Pterodactyl Rose *(1991)*

THE HOST

SELECTED POEMS

1965 — 1990

~ from ~

Depth of Field

(1970)

Birds and Roses are Birds and Roses

I have come to rely
on the timeless in the temporal,
on the always faithful inner-eye,
on detail that deepens to fond symbol.

But all morning the sun found
feathers scattered under a bush
where roses had fallen to the ground.
The remains of a thrush.

I would flesh this one bird's feathers,
resume its quick eye and lilting trill.
But these were not the mystics' flowers:
their bush cast a shadow like a bell.

The Bear

I

I was the first of us, leaving a downtown bar
one spring dusk, to see the bear.
I blamed it on beer.

It crossed the street to my side, deeper black
than the shut shops or near dark.
I tried to blink it back.

It passed an arm's length away. I stood straight
as a parking meter, and could scent
its long-slept lust.

I was the first of us to see the bear, the first to follow
its musky, rutting smell like a shadow
to its spring lair.

II

The beast's eyes glowed yellow on the stairs.
It rose to two legs and ripped its claws
across her shut door.

She led me quickly across her room, and bade
the enraged bear stand guard
beside her bed.

She pulled me down, and all the while
I felt its hot, fragrant muzzle,
until I heard her call

another to step inside the cage, the first to follow.
Later, the magic bear slept. As though
it could ever sleep another winter.

The Mower

No more stars are slashed from the hive
of heaven. The evening settles to stillness.
Today the wind's edges swept
the orchard like scythes. Now she rests.

Now the power mower,
drowsing in fumes of gasoline,
though all day her blades whirled
through windfalls under the apple trees,

though she was the great queen to bees
that rose from burrows in the fruit's flesh
to preen for her, to hear
her droning epithalamion,

neither dreams in her dark shed
nor sings mass for the dead, whose wings
are a scatter of stars on the cut grass.
She mows and rests in mindless monotone.

Existential

Half seeing and half smelling a scrap
of bacon, an eel blunts its nose on wire,
but finally steers into the cone of water
given shape by the trap.

Eats, and begins to define the rigid walls
of its cell. Burrows its mud floor, but bares
the same wire. The eel hovers, stares,
circles and settles.

It hears its gills feel the waters flow.
Waits in its cage. It can't or won't remember
the small way out it entered, or does know
and doesn't care, or neither.

The Insect

It never touches earth
though some say its legs
reach down just to the treetops
like rays of the sun.

It is transparent and takes on
the colors of the sky.
At night it is black. Stars
shine through it, the moon

draws it back and forth
like the tide. You have heard
the song of the wind
passing through its wings,

but cannot see it
as it floats above you
gliding on airstreams forever.
And it is huge. A plane

can pass between two cells
in its eye, a bird can fly
under it from morning to noon
and not pass it by.

It feeds on dust, woodsmoke,
blue clouds of vapor that rise
from the forests, everything the wind
carries. It never sleeps,

never tires, never dies.
You have thought its white shadow
moving across the ground
was the shadow of a cloud.

You have always known this.
You have always known the insect
is there. You are always
about to say its name.

The Dead

This evening's damp air
mutes even the crickets
used to scraping such shrill music.
The grass has fallen
almost to full dark.

I walk through flowerbeds,
inhaling the mixed perfumes
of black loam and moth-white mums,
through hedges to the row of dogwoods
blooming above the lawn:

their wash of pink blossoms seems
to float them in fathomless water,
like Monet's last lilies,
or Melville's rootless meadow
through which whales swim like scythes.

If this were the way the dead lost ground,
if the dead were drowned
in an evening's hushed, heavy air,
if the eyes of the dead branched
with an orchard of pink coral . . .

If this were death's kingdom,
if the eyes of the dead were not
a colorless blur,
if their blue bones
hummed beneath their stones . . .

Somewhere the May skies
rumble with thunder, flash
with edges of yellow lightning.
Something is about to happen,
as in the best paintings.

From the pond a field away,
bullfrogs croak to their log king.
What was it I
was thinking of saying?
I can't remember.

Depth of Field

The dew's weight is imperceptible
that gathers like a haze on the dark grass
and darkens imperceptibly the whorl
of threads in which the widow curls to pass

her night. Now the first shaft of sunlight
steers among the blades, touches and drums
taut by drying the edge of her vapor-white
web, now free to the low wind that strums

it alive. Unraveling her legs, hearing
her net sing the music of a dying fly
or violin of a gnat's feeble wing,
she rises to focus her hundreds of cells of eye

upon her field. And yet, within her sharp
geometry of sight, she is not angling
deep enough, or high. It is the harp
of the curved sun that orchestrates the morning.

The Stadium

The stadium is filled,
for this is the third night the moon
has not appeared as even a thin sickle.

We light the candles we were told to bring.
The diamond is lit red with torches.
Children run the bases.

A voice, as though from a tomb,
leads us to the last amen of a hymn.
Whole sections of the bleachers begin to moan.

The clergy files from the dugouts
to makeshift communion rails
that line the infield grass.

We've known, all our lives,
that we would gather here in the stadium
on just such a night,

that even the bravest among us
would weep softly in the dark aisles,
catching their difficult breath.

The King's Men

What is it, inside them and undeniable,
that mourns him? that drives them, searching
for the moon-shaped tracks of his horse,
a glint of armor within a maze of pines?

He'd known their barbarous need would never wane.
They will keep on to the next horizon,
where he waits. They will keep on, lowering
their barred visors against the setting sun.

Off the Hamptons

At night,
off the Hamptons,
the sky deceives with stars
long burnt out,

shellfish poachers
dig the forbidden waters
off the duck farms,
play hide-and-seek

with lawmen who slide
over the marshes in flatboats
like fish at the ocean's bottom,
one white ray of an eye

mounted on their foreheads.
Here the waters are poison,
the clams thick as diamonds
in the fables of lost mines.

Noise in the Trees

(1974)

I called to my boy, bidding him go out and see what noise this could be. The boy said: "The moon and stars are shining; the Milky Way glitters in the sky. Nowhere is there any noise of men. The noise must be in the trees."

— Ou-Yang Hsui

Dog Sacrifice at Lake Ronkonkoma

Now spears lift them by their ribs
over the black water to heaven.
Now they are almost dead.
Their eyes blaze in the moonlight,

as, all dark long,
the sacred lake laps shore
with syllables of approaching spring.
Men listen, the dogs stare and die, until,

Ronkonkoma, its curves a skull,
dreaming in its own bottomless bed,
fills with the first light of morning,
and the sun rises, clothed in the dogs' blood.

The Trail beside the River Platte

He saw, abandoned to the sand,
"claw-footed tables, once well waxed
and rubbed, or massive bureaus
of carved oak," now blistered,

sun-scorched, and warped.
So, the Ogillallah lived
as they had lived, rode
their ponies where the plains

were still humped black with buffalo —
enough, it seemed,
for the whole country
to feast on tongues, forever.

But the herds, of course, were doomed,
and the "large wandering communities"
that followed them would follow them
to nowhere. Parkman remembered

a day when innumerable animals thundered
into a ravine:
"Hoofs were jerked upwards," he said,
"tails flourished

in the air, and amid a cloud
of dust, the buffalo seemed
to sink into the earth
before me."

The Pigeons

Audubon watched the flocks beat by for days,
and tried, but could not count them:
their dung fell "like melting flakes of snow,"
the air buzzed until he lost his senses.

He heard, he said, their *coo-coo*
and *kee-kee* when they courted, and saw trees
of hundreds of nests, each cradling two
"broadly elliptical pure white eggs."

Over mast, they swept in "rich deep purple
circles," then roosted so thick that high limbs
cracked, and the pigeons avalanched
down the boughs, and had not room to fly,

and died by thousands. Kentucky farmers
fed their hogs on birds
knocked out of the air with poles. No net, stone,
arrow, or bullet could miss one,

so horses drew wagons of them,
and schooners sailed cargoes of them,
and locomotives pulled freightcars of them
to the cities where they sold for one cent each.

When you touched one, its soft
feathers fell away as easily as a puff
of dandelion seeds, and its delicate breast-
bone seemed to return the pulse of your thumb.

The Traffic

Red lights pulse and weave in
toward an accident ahead.
Trying to leave Smithtown,
I'm stopped dead,

here, where Whitman trooped
to tally the eighth-month flowers' bloom.
Diesels jam their bumpers together in a long line,
gas and rubber heat wafts in like soup.

A truck's exhaust curves up beside me
like a swan's neck. I sigh,
make a mistake, and breathe deep.
Concrete, signs, and cars cloud:

Lilacs utter their heart-shaped leaves,
locusts spell their shade. The Jericho's air
creaks with cartwheels, a carriage
moves with the certainty of mirage.

The Widow Blydenburgh flows to church,
stoops to admire an iris, and to smell.
A pigeon bends the slim branch of a birch.
The Widow plucks the iris for her Bible.

Horns soon blare me out of this.
Trailing a plume of smoke,
the trucker grunts his rig ahead.
I accelerate past a cop

directing traffic around the wreck.
He asks if I'm all right. I nod
and close the lane. Glass sparkles,
a splash of blood still shines

on the pavement, and time's itself again.
Pressed against the porch of Whitman's school,
the Dairy Freeze is booming, winks
its windows tinted green, and cool.

Where It Began

A few tides each summer
the soft skulls of jellyfish,
their tendons filtering the green water,
drift by thousands close to the Sound's shores.

A few tides each summer
spawns of sandworms choke the Sound,
pale blue, translucent, edged with blood,
bits of vein in the green water.

Worming at Short Beach

At Short Beach, reaching
   almost to the horizon, successions
      of sandbars lay bared

to the low tide, the furthest,
   toward which I walked
      over the wormgrounds,

toward which I waded
   through shallow sluices of channel,
      almost indistinct, and now blurred,

a small island of the mind
   I've tried to touch,
      define, and hold.

But I remember, as gulls worked
   the water's edge, ripped
      hermits from houses of shell,

or in my wake split
   the razors I threw aside,
      I remember, my back against

the sun's blaze, worming that far bar,
   forking close to clumps of sawgrass,
      turning the wet sand over,

breaking the worms' domains
   open to the dark sheen
      of my shadow.

My fork rasped against
   the shells of softclams
      that sprayed small geysers

as I dug, and the wind
   was a thin whisper of scythes
      over the waves. And now,

all this from a long time ago
   is almost lost
      and goes nowhere except deeper

year by year. But this was the way,
   when I worked that far bar,
      the light fell: the sandworms

were blood-red in my shadow,
  as I forked them
    into my shadow.

The Swan

The sun reached pond's edge, past false
lily of the valley smoldering
in deep shade,

past oaks scrawled with vines
dripping the ink tears
of wild grape,

reached to the end of a path lined with thistles,
to a cove defined by cattails, to kindle
the corpse of a swan:

whose bill was a tiger lily,
whose eyes burned blind
to the rising sun.

Wind rose to lift its quills, to fan
the white flames of its wings.
Dark water floated

the swan's neck, now curved limp
as a snake's shed skin.
I breathed

the pond's pollen, studied the water's haze
where spiders and sprites walked,
bugs swam circles,

pads curled their edges. At noon,
mud swirled and flowered,
the pond towed

the swan away: that said nothing, nothing
but the black light that flared
from its eyes as it sailed.

The Snapper

He is the pond's old father, its brain
and dark, permanent presence.
He is the snapper, and smells
rich and sick as a mat of weeds; and wears

a beard of leeches that suck frog, fish,
and snake blood from his neck; and drags
a tail ridged as though hacked out
with an ax. He rises: mud swirls

and blooms, lilies bob, water washes
his moss-humped back where, buried
deep in his sweet flesh, the pond ebbs
and flows its sure, slow heart.

The Return

I will touch things and things and no more thoughts.
— Robinson Jeffers

My boat slowed on the still water,
stopped in a thatch of lilies.
The moon leaned over the white lilies.

I waited for a sign, and stared
at the hooded water. On the far shore
brush broke, a deer broke cover.

I waited for a sign, and waited.
The moon lit the lilies to candles.
Their light reached down the water

to a dark flame, a fish: it hovered
under the pads, the pond held it
in its dim depths as though in amber.

Green, still, balanced in its own life,
breathing small breaths of light, this
was the world's oldest wonder, the arrow

of thought, the branch that all words
break against, the deep fire, the pure poise
of an object, the pond's presence, the pike.

The River

When, in the end,
we came to the river,
I hoped to float our wagon.
I remember
someone crying for help.
I never found out,
but it was not my wife,
my son, or my daughter — they
were safe beside me.
I pictured a woman trapped
in the wooden spokes of a wheel, turning
under the water, turning
back up to the air
to cry for her life.
I could not find her to help her.
But our wagon floated,
and we four knelt down
on the far shore.

I can still see the horses
breasting the current, their
wet rumps shining, their
black blinders flashing
in the slant sun.
I can still see my daughter
wrapping her arms about her brother
as he wraps her shawl
about her shoulders.
I can still see my wife's bonnet
filling in the wind,
and our wagon's canvas
filling in the wind.
Shouldn't I have known?
Later, the red sun
set in its east for the first time.

I should have known.
My life had deepened like a valley
to hold the river.
All my years the maples
tried to tell me, and the jays

that burned in the pineboughs
like blue flames,
and the winter pears
that hardened and reddened in the wind.
I should have known
that we would pass to the river,
that our wagon would float across it,
that we would kneel in the rich earth
of this shore, in this abiding dream, this
new life that will never cease
to nourish, or amaze.

The Lamb

Both hindlegs wrapped with rope,
Wenzel's chosen lamb hung head down
from a branch of one of his elms.

Its throat slashed, the lamb drained,
its nose and neckwool dripping,
lawn soaking up the bright blood.

Once skinned, once emptied of its blue
and yellow organs, its translucent
strings of intestines, and though its eyes

still bulged, the lamb rose
like steam from the pail of its guts,
toward stray shafts of sunlight

filtering through the trees. Until
it came to pass: I forgot my knees,
and entered the deep kingdom of death.

~ from ~

The Swastika Poems

(1977)

Riddle

From Belsen a crate of gold teeth,
from Dachau a mountain of shoes,
from Auschwitz a skin lampshade.
Who killed the Jews?

Not I, cries the typist,
not I, cries the engineer,
not I, cries Adolf Eichmann,
not I, cries Albert Speer.

My friend Fritz Nova lost his father —
a petty official had to choose.
My friend Lou Abrahms lost his brother.
Who killed the Jews?

David Nova swallowed gas,
Hyman Abrahms was beaten and starved.
Some men signed their papers,
and some stood guard,

and some herded them in,
and some dropped the pellets,
and some spread the ashes,
and some hosed the walls,

and some planted the wheat,
and some poured the steel,
and some cleared the rails,
and some raised the cattle.

Some smelled the smoke,
some just heard the news.
Were they Germans? Were they Nazis?
Were they human? Who killed the Jews?

The stars will remember the gold,
the sun will remember the shoes,
the moon will remember the skin.
But who killed the Jews?

The Trench

This is Verdun,
horizon of barbed wires
lit with flares.
Shudder of mortar on both flanks, and now
down the dreamed line the repeated scream:
gas. My thick fingers,
my mask unstraps slowly and heavily from my pack,
a fumble of straps,
buckles, tubes.
I try to hold my breath,
and now the mask is on,
smells of leather and honeysuckle vomit.
The poison smoke
drifts into the trench,
settles. My neck
strains to hold up the mask.
I will.
Behind this pane of isinglass
I am ready,
my bayonet fixed for the first black shape
to fill trenchlight above me and fall.
I know that all my life one
German soldier has plunged toward me
over the bodies of the lost.
I am ready for him.
We are both wearing masks,
and only one of us will live.

Darkness

Thirty, fifty, eighty years later,
it's getting darker.
The books read, the testimonies all taken,
the films seen through the eye's black lens,
darker. The words
remember: Treblinka green,
Nordhausen red,
Auschwitz blue, Mauthausen
orange, Belsen white —

colors considered
before those places named themselves. Thirty,
fifty, eighty years later. Now
the camps — I lose them —
where are they? Darker.
If it is true
that I've always loved him,
darker. If it is true
that I would kill again,
darker. If it is true
that nothing matters,
darker. If it is true
that I am jealous of them,
the Nazis' hooked crosses, the Jews' stripes . . .
He speaks inside me. Darker.
I lie on a table
in the Fuehrer's bunker,
outside his chamber,
in the hall. I am waiting.
They do not see me,
dogs nor people.
This dream begins again, film
circles and burns. Eighty, fifty,
thirty years. Darker. He
touched my forehead. He
speaks now, says, somehow,
lower, tells me to speak to the lower power,
for once, to say,
come back, enter, I was once alive.
Darker. The air
swims with words, hair
twines the words, numbers
along a wrist, along
a red brick shower. Darker.
To forgive them,
killer and victim. Darker.
Doctor, help me kill
the Goebbels children. Darker.
Across the street, now,
a cattlecar, stalled.
The skin lampshades darken under varnish.
Fragments. Can I call
him back? Millions still

call him back in deepest prayer,
but the light diffused
as spray, past
Andromeda, in spiral
shadows. Darker, always
darker. *SS*, death's head,
oval hollow deadface hole for boot —
fragments. The heroes
all dead in the first five minutes.
Darker. To enter
this darkness, to dig
this chancellery garden to my own
remains, to watch
as the black face and scrotum
lacking one egg stare up
at the sun, to speak
with that charred jaw,
carrying this with me. Darker.
Under the answer, under
the darkness, this love I have,
this lust to press these words. He
orders me *lower*,
and the black breastbone aches with it,
the last black liquid
cupped in the eyesockets smells of it,
odor of cyanide's bitter almond,
the viscera smeared to the backbone
shines with it, for me
to say it all, my
hands around his neck,
mouth to mouth, my lips
to kiss his eyes to sleep. We
will taste this history together,
my friend: take a deep breath.
Take it. Smell almond in the air.
The leader lives.

The Tree

    Not everyone can see the tree, its summer cloud of green
leaves or its bare radiance under winter sunlight. Not everyone
can see the tree, but it is still there, standing just outside the area

that was once a name and a village: Lidice. Not everyone can
see the tree, but most people, all those who can follow the
forked stick, the divining rod of their heart to the tree's place,
can hear it. The tree needs no wind to sound as though wind
blows through its leaves. The listener hears voices of children,
and of their mothers and fathers. There are moments of great
joy, music, dancing, but all the sounds of the life of Lidice:
drunks raving their systems, a woman moaning the old song of
the toothache, strain of harness on plowhorse, whistle of flail in
the golden fields. But under all these sounds is the hum of
lamentation, the voices' future.

The tree is still there, but when its body fell, it was cut up and
dragged away for the shredder. The tree's limbs and trunk were
pulped at the papermill. And now there is a book made of this
paper. When you find the book, when you turn its leaves, you
will hear the villagers' voices. When you hold the leaves of this
book to light, you will see the watermarks of their faces.

The Numinous

*Our language has no term that can isolate distinctly and
gather into one word the total numinous impression a thing
may make on the mind.*

— Rudolf Otto

We are walking a sidewalk
in a German city.
We are watching gray smoke
gutter along the roofs
just as it must have
from other terrible chimneys.
We are walking our way
almost into a trance.
We are walking our way
almost into a dream
only those with blue
numbers along their wrists
can truly imagine.

Now, just in front of us, something
bursts into the air.
For a few moments

our bodies echo fear.
Pigeons, we say,
only an explosion
of beautiful blue-gray pigeons.
Only pigeons that gather
over the buildings
and begin to circle.

We are walking again, counting
all the red poinsettias
between the windowpanes
and lace curtains.
It was only
a flock of pigeons:
we can still see them
circling over the block buildings,
a hundred hearts
beating in the air.
Beautiful blue-gray pigeons.
We will always remember.

Simple Truths

When a man has grown a body,
a body to carry with him
through nature for as long as he can,
when this body is taken from him
by other men and women who happen to be,
this time, in uniform,
then it is clear he has experienced
an act of barbarism,

and when a man has a wife,
a wife to love for as long as he lives,
when this wife is marked with a yellow star
and driven into a chamber she will never leave alive,
then this is murder,
so much is clear,

and when a woman has hair,
when her hair is shorn and her scalp bleeds,
when a woman has children,
children to love for as long as she lives,

when the children are taken from her,
when a man and his wife and their children
are put to death in a chamber of gas,
or with pistols at close range, or are starved,
or beaten, or injected by the thousands,
or ripped apart, by the thousands, by the millions,
it is clear that where we are
is Europe, in our century, during the years
from nineteen-hundred and thirty-five
to nineteen-hundred and forty-five
after the death of Jesus, who spoke of a different order,
but whose father, who is our father,
if he is our father,
if we must speak of him as father,
watched, and witnessed, and knew,

and when we remember,
when we touch the skin of our own bodies,
when we open our eyes into dream
or within the morning shine of sunlight
and remember what was taken
from these men, from these women,
from these children gassed and starved
and beaten and thrown against walls
and made to walk the valley
of knives and icepicks and otherwise
exterminated in ways appearing to us almost
beyond even the maniacal human imagination,
then it is clear that this is the German Reich,
during approximately ten years of our lord's time,

and when we read a book of these things,
when we hear the names of the camps,
when we see the films of the bulldozed dead
or the film of one boy struck on the head
with a club in the hands
of a German doctor who will wait
some days for the boy's skull to knit, and will enter
the time in his ledger, and then
take up the club to strike the boy again,
and wait some weeks for the boy's skull to knit,
and enter the time in his ledger again,
and strike the boy again,
and so on, until the boy, who,

at the end of the film of his life
can hardly stagger forward toward the doctor,
does die, and the doctor
enters exactly the time of the boy's death in his ledger,

when we read these things or see them,
then it is clear to us that this
happened, and within the lord's allowance, this
work of his minions, his poor
vicious dumb German victims twisted
into the swastika shapes of trees struck by lightning,
on this his earth, if he is our father,
if we must speak of him in this way,
this presence above us, within us, this
mover, this first cause, this spirit, this
curse, this bloodstream and brain-current, this
unfathomable oceanic ignorance of ourselves, this
automatic electric Aryan swerve, this

fortune that you and I were not the victims, this
luck that you and I were not the murderers, this
sense that you and I are clean and understand, this
stupidity that gives him breath, gives him life
as we kill them all, as we killed them all.

The Swastika Poems

They appeared, overnight,
on our steps, like frost stars
on our windows, their strict
crooked arms pointing

this way and that, scare-
crows, skeletons, limbs
akimbo. My father
cursed in his other tongue

and scraped them off,
or painted them over.
My mother bit her lips.
This was all a wonder,

and is: how that sign
came to be a star flashing
above our house when I dreamed,
how the star's bone-white light

first ordered me to follow,
how the light began
like the oak's leaves in autumn
to yellow, how the star now

sometimes softens the whole sky
with its twelve sides,
how the pen moves with it,

how the heart beats with it,
how the eyes remember.

Ewige Melodien

Something: dead friends' welcoming whispers? but
        something: wooden windbells, chimes? but
something: my skin soft now Lord we are all dead but

something: music lower than birdsong but
        something: our throats that screamed are soft now and
something: thrum of dew drying from grassblades? but

something: our fingers that clawed are soft now and
        something: rustle-of-grain sound somehow yellow? but
something: our lungs that burst with blood are soft now and

something: trees filling with windsong? but
        something: deep cello timbre, low resinous hum? but
something: jaw muscles soft now, neck muscles, tongues but

something: brain hymn, bodiless heartbeat? but
        something: we should have known this
something: . . . the melodies begin . . .

On an Archaic Torso of Apollo
(after Rilke)

We cannot experience that storied head
in which Apollo's eyeballs ripened like apples. Yet
his torso glows, candelabra by
whose beams his gaze, though screwed back low,

still persists, still shines. Or else his breast's
curve would never blind you, nor his loins'
slight arcs smile toward center-god, where
sperm seems candled from under.

Or else this stone would squat short, mute, dis-
figured under the shoulders' translucent fall,
nor flimmer the black light of a beast's pelt, nor

break free of its own ideas
like a star. For here there is nothing nowhere
does not see you, charge you: You must change your life.

~ from ~

Long Island Light

(1979)

Cardinals

When I was a kid I watched
Wenzel shoot them out of his appletrees,
those beautiful cardinals,
the males brighter than their mates,
and better targets.

All the summer's bees
tunnelled those bodies.
The redbirds' breastbones hummed,
the bees were that busy
among the windfalls.

One female lay eye-
high in a branch
as though alive,
though her eyes were closed.
When I walked into the tree,

when, with my thumb,
I touched her soft head-
feathers, a cap of skin
skimmed from her skull,
and I was happy.

When you and I hear
a call along the air,
one that is not pretty, that
does not trill or lilt,
should we trace it and kill it?

The Crane at Gibbs Pond

The boy stood by the darkening pond
watching the other shore.
Against pines,
a ghostly crane floated
from side to side,
crooning. Maybe
its mate had drowned. Maybe
its song lamented
the failing sun. Maybe

its plaint was joy,
heart-stricken praise
for its place of perfect loneliness. Maybe,
hearing its own echoing,
taking its own phantom gliding
the sky mirror of the pond
for its lost mother in her other world,
it tried to reach her
in the only way it could. Maybe,
as night diminished
all but the pond's black radiance,
the boy standing there knew
he would some day sing
of the crane, the crane's song,
and the soulful water.

This Father of Mine

I want to show you something
very beautiful, I say to my father
in this dream. We are walking
a tar road in Nesconset

around a slow bend
I still remember
where elms rose up
every evening of every summer

into great forests of darkness,
and blue-black birds swept
from one branch to another.
I want to show you something

very beautiful, I say, and take him
by his hand that never held
a book, his palm hardened
by boards and the handles

of a hundred hammers.
I notice sawdust
in the hair on his forearm.
I want to show you something

very beautiful. Now,
past the road's pebble and sand shoulder,
we step into oakbrush
where a path winds downward

to a pond I still remember.
In this dream the pond,
as it once was, is lipped
by ferns mirroring themselves

in green triangles
all along its edge.
On the far shore
a crane beats up out of the water,

curves over the trees,
hangs suspended
on its white wings
as though it were the white moon climbing

motionless in time
for as long as we stare. But
*I want to show you something
very beautiful,* I say to him,

and now, somehow, at the end
of the path of this dream,
we are barefoot, wading out
to knee-high water where

the pond's bottom disappears
into a depth I still remember.
There, I say to him,
and point down. But

from his pocket
he takes a handkerchief,
and stands, this father of mine,
knee-high in water in no hurry

wiping his glasses.
Over the far shore
the white crane still flies
to nowhere, motionless

as the white moon. But
there, I say, and point down, and now, at last,
we are looking down again
into the dream together,

into the pond's deepest beginnings,
into the place I remember
where elms rise toward surface
from the black water, from

thousands of fathoms, each leaf
distinct, each trunk furrowed
black and deep as a field
of plowed loam. *There*:

fish swim in the branches and bark valleys,
blue-black carp that vanish
and appear, and vanish again,
and appear. Their gills

glow red, their tails seem
to spray wakes of pale
yellow arcs as the fish vanish,
and appear, and vanish again, and appear.

Yes, he says, *yes*, and now
as though from his one word
spoken into the darkness of this dream,
the carp scatter

downward and outward
forever. And now that I have held
our two worlds together
for as long as this, the day,

in the whitest light we have ever seen,
rises from the bottom of the water through the elms.
It is over, I think,
though I almost remember

that we hold hands again,
and talk for the first time,
and walk toward home,
which is far away.

Anthem

I descended once
  into madness where
    a bell does swing above its rope,

the spinal column,
  a low lead reverberation,
    the struck sound spaced vertebrae apart.

My carpenter father's gluepot filled,
  again, with sawdust.
    Broken, bearing his pockets'

emptiness behind his eyes,
  he washed his hands in our narrow kitchen,
    my mother screaming, "Where's our money,

where's our money?" I watched them
  slam themselves into their rusted Ford
    and drive away. Then

that bell began. Was it real? Had its waves
  carried to our lawn
    from miles away where,

betrayed, dead, my Jesus lay suspended
  in robes of stained glass, but about to rise
    into the sun's rays?

But this was not my church:
  I listened to the bell
    toll syllables of madness while

the real sun's spectrum and glisten
  rushed out of a huge backyard elm
    like a sunburst in reverse.

I remember running with the bell
  into the back woods —
    brush-slash and blood until

all color returned to the world.
  That bell diminished,
    and I who had heard its call to darkness,

the death knell, I who had entered the vacuum
  that drew all light at mid-day
    out of the great tree,

I who had found that country
  where my parents sang
    "Give us money, money, money,

or give us death, O America,"
  walked out of the woods as they died.

Of Gatsby

Night, "wings beating in the trees."
Now Nick sees he isn't alone:
fifty feet away his neighbor trembles
and stretches his arms out toward the bay:
a green light shines over
the Island's mysterious water
like a mirage of emerald fire.
But Gatsby cannot be approached.
Soon, as though he were never there,
Gatsby is gone.

But in his deepest scene Gatsby decides
to name his name.
He taps at Nick's door in the rain
until it opens wider
than his whole life can bear.
After an impossible hello again
to the golden girl of his own composition,
he leans against a mantle, almost
knocking a dead clock to the floor.
Fitzgerald knew that this was time
for tears: Gatsby will take her home,
their hearts will begin to kindle,
she'll cry into a pile of his shirts.

In the raw sunlight when the year
turned for one last season
to gray woodsmoke and ashes,
Gatsby's blood touched the water red.
Nick returned to stocks and bonds,
and she, since she could not be there
to save the forsaken dreamer
from his dream, just disappeared.

Only we are left
to drive his opulent driveway once or twice,
to know his house like no one else.

For the Year 2500

        In Long Island's sand, my fingers
    found this talisman,
this small tri-
    angular deer skull
        to hold to your eye.

        Within its milky glow
    against the sun, notice
the thin brainpan's curved
    veins of whiter bone, the white
        wheel spokes, the radiant

        creation, the crystalline-based
    star-pattern born
in the Word, in water, in sperm.
    Every skull holds our sun's first fires.
        Your dead Lord lives at the wheel's hub.

Witness

We'd walked into the small warm shed
where spring lambs lay in straw
in the half-dark still smelling of their birth,
of ammonia, the damp grass, dung,
into this world in the middle of a field
where lambs bleating soft songs lifted
their heavy heads toward their mothers,
gentle presences within their wool clouds.
Later, outside, as I watched,
Wenzel wrapped his left arm around a sheep's neck
and struck her with the sledge in his right hand.
The dying sheep, her forehead crushed, cried out,
past pain, for her mortal life. Blood flowed
from her burst skull, over her eyes, her black nose.

Wenzel dropped her to the grass.
When I ran home, I struck my head
on a blossoming apple-bough.
Where was the dead sheep?
What did I hear?
Where is the witness now?

I was nine or ten.
Her cry was terror,
so I lay awake to hear her,
to wonder why she didn't seem to know
her next manger, her golden fields.
Her odors drifted through my screen —
the hay at the roots of her wool,
her urine, the wet graindust under her chin,
her birth fluids hot and flecked with blood.
I could hear her bleat
to her last lamb, hear her heartbeat
in the black air of my room.
Where was the dead sheep?
Why did she cry for her loss?
Where is the witness now?

Not to accept, but to awaken.
Not to understand, to cry terror, but to know
that even a billion years later, now,
we breathe the first circle of light,
and the light curves into us, into the deer's back,
the man's neck, the woman's thigh,
the cat's mouse-mossed tongue, all the ruby
berries ripening in evening air.
The dead elms and chestnuts are of it, and do not
break the curve. The jeweled flies sip it,
and do not break the curve.
Our homes inhabit, and ride the curve.
Our moon, our rivers, the furthest stars blinking blue,
the great named and nameless comets do not break the curve.
The odorous apple-blossom rain does not break the curve.
The struck ewe's broken brainpan does not break the curve.
Wenzel nor this witness breaks the curve.

In the shed's dusk where spring lambs
sang to their mothers, in my dark room
where the dead ewe's odors drifted my sleep,
and now, within these cells where her forehead blood

flows once more into recollection,
the light curves. You and I bear witness, and know this,
and as we do the light curves into this knowledge.
The struck ewe lives in this light,
in this curve of the only unbroken light.

Fires

> *The prairies burning form some of the most beautiful scenes*
> *that are to be witnessed in the country, and also some of the*
> *most sublime.*
>
> — George Catlin

I

Where, on prairie elevations,
    grass clings thin, sparse, as low
        as in what Easterners would call a meadow, no
animal fears the gentle fire it smells

from far away. Sometimes invisible,
    the burn's feeble flame
        travels to the eye as only its black line,
and when they must, as they must each autumn

when lightning seems to strike off
    yellow sections of itself
        lateral across this land,
the wild bodies who know fire

will wait for it to tongue their lairs,
    will step over it or walk through it
        across the warm cinders
to another year. At night, the flame's

luminous blue wavery liquid edge
    pours over the sides and tops
        of bluffs in chains, "hanging suspended,"
as George Catlin put it in 1830,

"in graceful festoons from the skies."
    With him, we could watch this nightfire
        for a long time: even the stars appear
to rise from ground that the sinuous

soft flame blackens behind it.
   With him, we could watch this nightfire
      for a long time, bed down
on the still-warm ground behind it,

and sleep, the waving
   flames receding
      in grasshead sparkles
like Andromeda, or a dream.

II

But Catlin knew that the place came
   for us to stand erect
      in our mounts' stirrups, to stare for fire
over the tall cover of flatland grass,

in other country, along the Missouri,
   the Platte, the Arkansas.
      To be caught here is to die:
pea-vines tangle the eight-foot grasses,

fire drives smoke before it, booms
   terror into the horses rearing up in circles:
      the leaping flames soon surround
to take all horsehair and flesh

in screams and thunderous noise. We
   would not be the first. Whole
      parties of Indians, herds
of buffalo and deer have burned into a charred meal

only ants are left alive to eat, and the roots
   of next spring's prairie. These scenes
      roll with black smoke and streaks of red,
both beautiful and sublime, as the painter said.

III

Those galaxies, each at least one hundred
   billion bodies falling away from us,
      one hundred billion, ten to the eleventh power,
billions dead and invisible already —

that is the far darkness. Planets
   burn out, turn, for all we know,
      into ice, or cold moons, if anything only an unseen
trace of fern or beings in fossil to prove perished fire,

but here, for now, on this earth,
     even for those creatures whose marrow
          boiled within their bones
and through whose ribs the prairie wind

tuned itself to its own truth,
     even for these the fires sear
          something else. Just now, within this revery of him,
not knowing, as in all of Catlin's paintings,

how to end this, or where, of its own discord, it does,
     I looked up again out
          of my twentieth-century window
over my left shoulder:

Catlin's West is dead, yes, in its own way,
     but the same sun's unimaginable power drives suburban
          and miraculous through flowers banked
against these houses, flames the black-flecked slashed vivid

undiminished orange heads of tiger lily, and even the most
     domestic geranium along a front border
          bursts with spots of fire red
as the open mouths of horses trapped in that other world.

IV

If much of this is sad, this
     necessary "civilized
          wilderness"
our minds have made for us,

still the fires kindle and begin,
     somewhere beneath the breastbone,
          somehow under the lungs,
radiate from rooftops,

the sunlit concrete,
     brick, even the black
          macadam to abdomen and groin, begin,
in their last stages, to leap up

into the city, into the brain's
     nerves and grasses, out
          into the fingers' touch, even
into love. Catlin's West is lost, except

we still feel these fires, by night
   a necklace blue as a glass snake in the heavens,
     by day as flickering sun
tongues its way along a walk, the flash of steel

smokestacks, or in lightning, or the rains'
   rolling fog, at sunset
     in the burnished clouds rising
over lines of trees rising

over lines of buildings still
   burning, outside, within,
     with wild and elemental meanings
from our living sun.

The Ewe

Ropes to her hind legs and the elm's branch
held her just above the ground in silhouette.
I'd almost run into her, but veered away in time,
and now knelt out of range
of her bulbous eyes, her cavernous ribcage.

I was alone, stared, and the dead ewe,
plane of silver flesh and flesh-shadowed bone
flamed into light, flew downward into the ground,
and disappeared. When, from this other world,
she rose into silhouette again,

I crawled closer, as I remember,
looked up into her eyes, and entered. . . .
And last night, kneeling within a dream
under her eyes again, I entered, and here,
in this cave of silence, at the poised

center of being, in the ewe's skull,
I received her light, but the human
power of color, the sunset lavenders,
the moon-silvered meadow,
the curved sledge burst with stars.

~ from ~

The City Parables

(1980)

The City Parables

These tallow- and meat-
covered hooks roped to lamp posts:
some will take them

into themselves almost deeper
than their lives can bear,
and lunge, tearing themselves apart,

hearing their own retched snarls,
seeing their own blood smoking across the sidewalks,
these hooks in their breastbones,

their brainfires gusting
bright or black as this city
receives them, repels them

The Child

In my dream, I saw the Christ child.
I knew, then, that He was true:
His halo swam with blue,
translucent fish made only of light.

I walked outside.
In the deepening evening, stars
streaming script across the heavens,
I cut my wrists and died while saying

"Lord, I am this happy, I must
come to You now. . . ." I believe,
as this morning breaks,
He receives me: I can see,

again, that stable, those beasts
huffing vapor into the straw-
gold air, that child of dream
drawing me dying to His side.

The Sunflower

Soon, at wood's edge, the single
sunflower I'd planted opened to full bloom.
Careless, I'd pass by, and pass again, until
an evening darkness of drenched loam

when I returned, by accident, or drawn there.
Around its center, small petals glowed gold,
yes, and real, but this time another color
silenced me as I knelt and stared upward,

as the sunflower's crook-necked head
imploded the shine
blacker than absence. Locked
in its meditation,

I bore witness as night wind,
leaves, all birdsong and moonlight
broke up, poured
over the petal edge. I managed

prayer aloud,
but each syllable entered
the same abyss. To live, for now, I lifted
from my knees, hearing my last word

drift into the dead world
of vacuum and sunflower head, *Lord, lord* . . .

The Buffalo

Had the herds roamed the moon,
we could have seen them
in the clear night sky,

rivers of black light
flowing and emptying
into the sea.

The Host

In the dying pond,
under an oilspilled rainbow where
cement clumped, cans rusted, and slick tires
glinted their whitewall irises,
at the edge where liquid congealed,
a lump of mud shifted.
I knew what it was,
and knelt to poke it with a wire
from the saddest mattress in the world.

Maybe a month out of its rubbery egg,
the young snapper hid,
or tried to, drew back its head,
but algae-scum outlined its oval shell,
its ridged chine diminished
toward its tail,
and I lifted the turtle
into the air, its jaws open,
its crooked neck unfolding upward.

It twisted, could not reach me.
I found out its soft, small undershell where,
already, a leech lodged
beneath its left hindleg, sucking
some of whatever blood
its host could filter from the pond, its host.
They would grow together, if the snapper lived.
Its yellow eyes insisted it would.
I gave it back to the oil sludge

where it was born, and watched it
bury itself, in time, and disappear. . . .
I'd like to leave it living there,
but churned slime above it blurs, burns,
bursts into black glare, every atom
of chemical water, rust residue, planet vomit
shining in deathlight. The snapper's
bleached shell ascends the 21st century,
empty, beyond illusion.

The Conspiracy

We were several in the middle of the ocean.
We'd been there a full calendar, our boat tied to a tree.
In swells of water and cloud,
some stairs, the end of a dock, pulled apart.

The others decided on the boat, and cut the rope.
They drifted away, their motor gulping and sobbing,
taking its oil fumes with them.
I couldn't see your face, but you were with me

in the stout, lower branches of our tree,
an oak rooted in the rising water. . . .
I could tell, by the leaves
shading us and shedding breakers,

that it was summer. We would live. That city,
that conspiracy, all those bastards in the boat would drown.
Warm in the tree's gray-green shadow,
if only for one more season,

we'd be safe here, would catch and eat
minnows that schooled in the roots of our oak.
We'd sleep in the tree, and wait,
counting fins cutting the air around us.

A Bridge

(for Han)

Driving through rain over the Brockport bridge
of the Erie Canal, wipers sweeping
half-moons on the windshield,
I was lost to this small town:

I remembered Rome, our dash
across cobblestones to stand
under the Pantheon's massive portico.
We knew where we were, and walked inside, alone.

This is the way life happens:
all around us, Italy's kings kept secret counsel,
but rain, as it had since Hadrian, swept in
where the dome opens on purpose to the sky.

"Imagine," you said, and that was all.
We held hands and leaned against
a yellow marble ledge
near Raphael, and listened.

Where were we?
Where are we now?
Soon the rain rose, and light washed in,
as it does, in one of Raphael's own paintings.

Off the Expressway

In the evening meadow, whorls of gray mist.
Within the mist, a deer, a doe, almost
disembodied. She lifts her head from clover.
She knows she's in danger, and will be, forever,

because of what we say, or how we see,
or how we hear her: the meadow is poetry,
the deer its object
and elusive music, the mist

her safety should we try to track and kill her.
Now the poem's traffic spirits us away.
The expressway ends in the city, gray
with mist, through which dreamers walk, and deer.

A Story from Chekhov

Gleb Smirnoff, surveyor, hires the huge peasant Klim
to take him to Devkino, through fifty miles of darkness.
The gaunt pony and rude wagon groan,
witch voices in the winter wilderness.

Gleb begins to fear the broad-backed Klim,
raves of his own miraculous strength,
claims two, three revolvers in his pockets!
But now he has frightened Klim, who jumps down

and runs away. . . . Gleb, helpless fool, fowl
in this world of wolves, gooseflesh
stippling his spine, sings, quietly, all night long,
"Klim, come back. I lied. I was afraid.

Klim . . . Klim . . ." At last,
the longed-for peasant appears again.
Gleb orders/begs him to take the reins.
Listen to their hearts through the darkness to Devkino.

Mantle

      Mantle ran so hard, they said,
      he tore his legs to pieces.
      What is this but spirit?

52 homers in '56, the triple crown.
I was a high-school junior, batting
   fourth behind him in a dream.

I prayed for him to quit, before
his lifetime dropped below .300.
   But he didn't, and it did.

He makes Brylcreem commercials now,
models with open mouths draped around him
   as they never were in Commerce, Oklahoma,

      where the sandy-haired, wide-shouldered boy
   stood up against his barn,
      lefty for an hour (Ruth, Gehrig),

      then righty (DiMaggio),
   as his father winged them in,
      and the future blew toward him

         now a fastball, now a slow
         curve hanging
            like a model's smile.

Redwings

Maybe you've noticed that around here
red-winged blackbirds aren't rare,
but aren't seen often, either, and then, at distance,
banking away from roads as we pass.

But one morning, I saw a hundred,
more, feeding on seed I'd scattered
under a line of pines planted
more than a hundred years before.

Almost at rest, their feathers folded close,
only yellow wingbars
break their black bodies. But when, as they did,
all at once, they lifted, that *red* . . .

I've tried for a long time, and maybe should,
to tell you how the disembodied redwings
flared and vanished.
I've lost them in every telling.

So much for me. I could die now, anyway.
Could you? We will close our eyes
and rest, in case the blackbirds, in slow motion,
assume again the flames they are, and rise.

Emblem

I walked outside from where I'd written,
again, decades after walking Belsen, a weak cry.
Darkness, forgetfulness, no stars,
only my own eyes to close, or open. Then,
above the meadow where I stood, one firefly
spoke its tiny light, and then others,
as far as I could see. This earth is not an emblem
of the dead, I warned myself inside this dream.
The fireflies brightened, joined, became the sun.

Plague Sermon

Some were for fires, but not coal,
but wood fires for the city,
whole forests of fires
carted into the city,
some for the turpentine effluvia
of fir and cedar, some for wetted pine
billowing life-saving smoke,
some for oak's skin-basting
pustule-drying heat. No
use. What is the wood
under *your* breastbone?

Mornings and evenings
wagons made their rounds:
Bring out your dead. We tried,
the funerals becoming so many
we could not toll the bell,
mourn, weep, wear aught
but black, or make coffins.

Grass grew in the desolate streets,
wind shattered windows
in empty houses; the stricken
left their beds by night to make
moonlit silhouettes of antic gesture,
laugh, speak to trees or dogs,
reign as king or queen of Britain
for an hour, or curse the church,
or leap into the Thames.
What is *your* faithful song?

Bring out your dead. And we did.
And you who hear this,
centuries hence,
but under aegis of the same
circular Providence,
you who harbor the pestilence within,
bring out your dead.

~ from ~

Lord Dragonfly

(1981)

Lord Dragonfly

i.

A friend dies.
Another,
forcing the lilac to flower.

ii.

In a corner of the field, wild
grapevine climbs a lightning
groove in the ash trunk.
Where are the dead?

iii.

In the field's drizzle and gloom,
soft-glowing sheaths,
the souls of spikes
of goldenrod.

iv.

Breaking the field I find
a ring of round white stones,
gift of the glacier.

v.

As I dig, the old apple stump
tries pulling itself deeper
by its last root.

vi.

Inside the windfall apple
tunnels of bees
singing.

vii.

I'm glad,
grasshopper of my childhood,
you've grown your legs back.

viii.

Pure white found
a wild rose to live in,
for now.

ix.

Half the mantis still
prays on my scythe blade.

x.

In the mowed field,
a million crickets for hire.
My steps are money.

xi.

My wife away.
In a garden furrow,
I find her lost earring.

xii.

Lord Dragonfly
sees me from all sides
at once.

xiii.

Pear blossoms
sift the same air
as last year.

xiv.

No one has ever
seen snow fall here,
until next year.

xv.

The hummingbird whirrs,
only its ruby
throat feathers clear.

xvi.

Curves of the summer pepper
lit with every green.

xvii.

With trees overhead,
where is the void?

                  xviii.

                  One red cardinal,
                  one gray cardinal,
                  three cinnamon-spotted eggs.

xix.

I am safe here,
not a friend in sight.

         xx.

         I lean on my shovel,
         trusting the field.

                  xxi.

                  Playing dead,
                  Japanese beetles tumble
                  from a skeleton leaf.

xxii.

Already morning glory
tendrils circle
my shovel's handle.

xxiii.

Beneath its tassels
an ear of corn
erupts in fungus,
the blackest light.

xxiv.

When I look for him,
he is away,
finding another home,
the borer that killed my poplar.

xxv.

Prune for shade.

xxvi.

Rooted,
the trees are green islands
in fog
in the shifting field.

xxvii.

Sunflower, my lamp,
on such a rainy day.

xxviii.

Tree-man
carrying branches
of silver maple
I walk through the storm.

xxix.

Evening: time to level
the frantic anthill,
the field's brain.

xxx.

Meteor shower —
a little more, or less,
of the Lord.

xxxi.

Outside at night
I close my eyes:
the lost chestnuts' roots
luminous underground.

xxxii.

This western corner of the field,
this grove of ash —
if there were a place . . .

      xxxiii.

      Beetle's cargo:
      heaviness?
      happiness?
      Neither, nor
      both together.

xxxiv.

In the far galaxies,
collapsed stars,
yes, but here,
light escapes
even the blackberries.

xxxv.

In the autumn field,
my body,
a warm stone.

      xxxvi.

      Cosmos, planet, field,
      and the dead
      aware of everything!

Evening Dawning

i.

A crow's black squawk —
my white field lost again.

ii.

All bone,
feet numb,
rhythm gone,
I clod across the field.

    iii.

    From the outer world,
    a siren, and a dog's
    painsong.

iv.

In high snow,
which way the root,
which way the tip
of the bramble arch?

v.

Sparrow hearts
criss-crossing
the frozen field.

    vi.

    In the long, lowest needles
    of white pine,
    a message,
    frozen in urine.

vii.

White moon shell,
and a single gull
flying toward me
from shore.

    viii.

    Upswirl, sudden
    white-out.
    My cabin within,
    I close my eyes to find it.

ix.

My footprints already
in front of me,
I walk toward the other world.

x.

Bowing,
I address the door,
pray, once more,
for that opening
to everywhere,
and enter.

xi.

Pine chair cold,
hands cold,
mind cold
and ready.

xii.

World, mind, words —
wax, wick, matches.

xiii.

Under my cabin,
field mice,
and China.

xiv.

To see the white sea,
I and my old pen knife
scrape a porthole
in the frosted window.

xv.

Rabbit tracks,
rabbit pellets,
my own footsteps
drifting with snow.

xvi.

What kind of blood
in the red-twig dogwood?

xvii.

They disappear,
St. Francis now a spruce
receiving sparrows
into his dark boughs.

xviii.

Logic, logic —
trillions of intricate hexagons.

xix.

From another time
at field's edge
the first ash
veiled in a dream
in falling snow.

xx.

Cardinal,
mote of male blood
in the winter ash.

xxi.

Under the snow,
infinitesimal pearls,
insects speeding
to summer.

xxii.

Already ferns
frost my window.

xxiii.

I am thirty-eight.
Evening is dawning.

xxiv.

Lord, winter,
I place this cabin
in your begging bowl.

xxv.

Dying, the brain
sheds cells.
In the end,
perfect numbers,
the mind,
the Milky Way's stars.

xxvi.

Candlebeam and dust,
river and fish,
as long as they last.

xxvii.

Blue stars in the blue snow
over the elm stump.

xxviii.

In the window,
holding out his pale arms,
my dead friend,
above, within, beyond the field.

xxix.

I have come to have
everything, but now
the miserable
weep in chapels
under the spruce boughs.

xxx.

Even winter evenings
spores of black knot, killer
of cherry, plum, and apple,

xxxi.

mindless, invisible,
drift over the field,
but will anchor.

xxxii.

Verdun, Belsen, Jonestown — still,
from indwelling darkness, human
music, a summons
to praise.

xxxiii.

A boy, I killed these sparrows
whose *tsweet, tsweet* now
enters my cabin,
forgiving everything.

xxxiv.

I still hear
the summer woodpecker, red
godhead hammering holes
into my heartwood.

xxxv.

How long have I been here,
scent of pinesap
flowing through my chair?

xxxvi.
Snow clouds,
Milky Way nowhere in sight,
moon hidden, all earth gone —
there is a life, this one,
beyond the body.

~ from ~

Erika

(1984)

Stories

I

A few hours before Heinrich,
my father's father, drowned in the North Sea
in nineteen-twenty at twenty-eight, he
walked outside his small home at Aurich

to pack his nets, spread on hedges to dry
in the German sun. My father, ten,
helped double, and double them again,
hand to hand, eye to blue eye

with his father who would soon be dead.
The horse-drawn wagon drew away. The fisherman
waved farewell to his wife and three sons.
My father, as he always did, tossed

an apple to the rider who, this morning,
backlit, rode silhouette against the sun.
Heinrich's shade dropped the apple, the fortune
in eel, fluke, and mackerel it meant to bring.

This simple world of signs went on. The wind-ripped
brine-tinged fields lay fallow, small flounders
dozed at low tide under the stars
in the mud flats until, at daylight, speared

by children. The hollow, the shadow, the dead whine,
the wrack father twisting at anchor in my father's chest,
the North Sea's black shine, the North Wind's lost
song, the painful windfalls — these diminished, but that son

who planed thin the blades of his father's ash oars
and mounted them where they have pointed fifty years
into the wind above that house — arrow, weathervane —
would be no fisherman. Now, on their way down

to the same ancestral sea,
the luckier Aurich sons know that Heinrich's soul
lives in the wind, his only home,
in the seawind. This is one story.

II

I remember walking with my father
near the blue spruce that smoldered in shade,

hunched and crushed at an edge of wood,
but alive in the blocked Long Island light. He bent over

to tie the shoe I lifted to his knee.
I was so close, this once, that when
he looked up, I saw his left pupil widen,
fill with the blue-tipped green-black tree,

and swell with tears. When I dream of this,
I know, as I couldn't then, his two brothers
are just dead. I cup his tears
in my palm, as I didn't then, and the spruce

rises, from this water,
so blue, so light I am able to hold it
above us. The tree's perfect
form branches above us. This is another.

III

Wilhelm was killed in Holland,
Hermann over Russia. The North Sea's spawn
did not miss a rhythm when Berlin
burned to the ground.

What if the world is filled with stories? —
we hear only a few, live fewer,
and most that we live or hear
solve nothing, lead nowhere; but the spruce

appears again, rooted in dreamed tears,
yes, each branch, each needle
its own true story, yours,
mine, ours to tell.

Kotov

Ivan Ivanovitch Kotov, short of speech,
clarity drifting away to mindlessness —
Kotov of stutter and suddenly empty eyes —
only Kotov, in all Russia, of all those locked inside,
survived the *dushegubka*,
the murder wagon, the gas van. Only Kotov,

pushed with his new bride
into the seatless seven-ton gray truck,
stood on that grated floor, and lived. Only Kotov,
pressed together with fifty others, would wake
in the ditch of dead, half buried, and crawl away.
He'd smelled gas, torn off one sleeve,
soaked it in his urine, covered nose and mouth,

lost consciousness, and lived, waking
in a pit of bodies somewhere outside of Krasnodar.
His wife? — he could not find her.
Except for the dead, he was alone. . . .
He stood up, staggered and groped through fields
back to the city, where he hid until the end.

Only Kotov, saved by his own brain and urine, woke
from that wedding in the death van,
in Russia, in the time of that German invention,
the windowless seven-ton gray *dushegubka*.

The Trains

Signed by Franz Paul Stangl, Commandant,
there is in Berlin a document,
an order of transmittal from Treblinka:

248 freight cars of clothing,
400,000 gold watches,
25 freight cars of women's hair.

Some clothing was kept, some pulped for paper.
The finest watches were never melted down.
All the women's hair was used for mattresses, or dolls.

Would these words like to use some of that same paper?
One of those watches may pulse in your own wrist.
Does someone you know collect dolls, or sleep on human hair?

He is dead at last, Commandant Stangl of Treblinka,
but the camp's three syllables still sound like freight cars
straining around a curve, Treblinka,

Treblinka. Clothing, time in gold watches,
women's hair for mattresses and dolls' heads.
Treblinka. The trains from Treblinka.

Poem Touching the Gestapo

> *Behind the apparently iron front of Teutonic organization, there
> was a sort of willed chaos.*
>
> — Edward Crankshaw

> *The system of administration [at Auschwitz] was completely
> without logic. It was stupefying to see how little the orders
> which followed one another had in common. This was only
> partly due to negligence.*
>
> — Olga Lengyel

You now, you in the next century, and the next,
hear what you'll almost remember,
see into photos where he still stands, Himmler,
whose round and puffy face concealed visions,

cortege of the condemned winding toward Birkenau,

and how to preserve Jews' heads in hermetically sealed tins,

der Ritter, knight, *treuer Heinrich*,

visions of death's head returning in Reich's light,
the Aryan skull ascending the misformed skull of the beast,
the Jew, Gypsy, lunatic, Slav, syphilitic, homosexual,

ravens and wolves, the Blood Flag, composer Wagner
whose heart went out to frogs, who, like Martin Luther,
wanted to drive Jews "like mad dogs out of the land,"

Heydrich dead but given Lidice,
Mengele injecting dye into Jewish eyes —
Ist das die deutsche Kultur? —
this vomit at last this last
cleansing and an end to it,
if it is possible, if I will it now,

Lebensborn stud farms, *Rassenschande, Protocols
of the Elders of Zion, SS* dancing in nuns' clothes,

Otto Ohlendorf, who left his Berlin desk to command
Einsatsgruppe D and roam the East killing
one million undesirables in less than two years' time,
lamenting the mental strain on his men,
the stench of inadequate graves,
corpses that fouled themselves in the gas vans,

graves rupturing, backs, backs of heads, limbs
above ground as they are here, if I will it now,
the day-in, day-out shootings of Jews, some attractive,
brave, even intelligent, but to be dealt with
in strict military order, not like at Treblinka where
gas chambers were too small, and converted gas vans' engines
sometimes wouldn't start, the thousands already
packed into the showers for history,

their hands up so more would fit, and smaller children
thrown in at the space left at the top,
and we knew they were all dead, said Hoess of Auschwitz,
when the screaming stopped,

Endlösung, Edelweiss, *Lebensraum, Mussulmen, Cyklon B,*

"and his large blue eyes like stars," as Goebbels wrote,
and the Fuehrer's films of conspirators on meathooks,

we cannot keep it all, an end to it,
visions of loyal Heinrich, what engineer Grabe saw at Dubno,
he and two postmen allowed to watch, the vans arriving,
a father holding his boy and pointing to that sky,
explaining something, when the SS shouted and counted off
twenty more or less and pushed them behind the earth mound,

Stahlhelm, Horst Wessel, Goering in a toga at *Karinhalle*,
redbeard Barbarossa rising,

that father and son, and the sister remembered by Grabe
as pointing to herself, slim girl with black hair,
and saying, "twenty-three years old,"
as Grabe behind the mound saw a tremendous grave,

the holy orders of the SS, Lorelei, the Reichstag fire,
Befehl ist Befehl, Anne Frank in Belsen, jackboots, Krupp,

bodies wedged together tightly on top of one another,
some still moving, lifting arms to show life,
the pit two-thirds full, maybe a thousand dead,
the German who did the shooting sitting at the edge,
his gun on his knees, and he's smoking a cigarette,
as more naked victims descend steps cut in the pit's clay,
clamber over the heads of those already dead there,
and lay themselves down. Grabe heard some speak
in low voice . . . listen . . .

before the shooting, the twitching, the spurting blood,
competition for the highest extermination counts,
flesh sometimes splashed on field reports,
seldom time even to save skulls with perfect teeth
for perfect paperweights,

his will be done, and kill them, something deeper dying,
but kill them, cognac and nightmares but kill them,
Eichmann's "units," the visions, the trenches
angled with ditches to drain off the human fat,

the twins and dwarfs, the dissidents *aus Nacht und Nebel*,

Professor Dr. Hans Kramer of the University of Munster
who stood on a platform to channel new arrivals —
gas chamber, forced labor, gas chamber — and later,
in special action, saw live women and children thrown into pits
and soaked with gasoline and set on fire —
Kramer, a doctor, who kept a diary filled with
"excellent lunch: tomato soup, half a hen with
potatoes and red cabbage, sweets and marvelous vanilla ice,"
while trains kept coming, families with

photograph albums falling out of the cars, the books
of the camps and prisons, the albums imprinting the air,
as here, we close our eyes, and the rain falling from photos
onto the earth, dried in the sun and raining again,
no way to them now but this way, willed chaos,

visions deeper in time than even the graves of the murdered
daughter who tells us her age,
in the round face of the man with glasses and weak chin,
Himmler, *Geheime Staats Polizei*, twisting his snake ring,

as now the millions approach, these trucks arriving with more,
these trains arriving with more, from *Prinz Albrecht Strasse*,
from the mental strain on Ohlendorf's men,
from the ravine at Babi Yar, from the future,
from the pond at Auschwitz and the clouds of ash,
from numberless mass graves where Xian prayer and Kaddish
now slow into undersong, O Deutschland, my soul, this soil
resettled forever here, remembered, poem touching the Gestapo,
the families, the children, the visions,
the visions . . .

The Legacy

I am alive.   Those Jews are dead.
I am living.   They are dead.
I think of them.   They are dead.
I think of them.   They are dead.
I think of one.   He wants to speak.
I think of him.   He makes a sound.
I hear his sound.   He moans.
I hear him moan.   He is dying.
I am alive.   He is dying.
I am living.   They are dying.
I think of them.   They are dead.
I think of one.   She is dead.
I think of her.   She makes a sound.
I hear her sound.   She makes an r sound.
I hear her sound.   She repeats the r.
I remember them.   They are dead.
I remember his moan.   He is dead.
I remember her r.   She is dead.
I remember them.   They make sounds.
I remember them.   They die.
I remember them.   They are making sounds.
I dream of them.   They sing.
I hear them sing.   They sing together.
I hear their song.   Their song is mine.
I smell of almond.   They smell of almond.
I die with them.   They live with me.
I leave to meet them.   They come to meet me.
I am dying.   They are living.
I am dying.   They are singing.
I am dead.   They are living.
I am dead.   They are singing.
I am dead.   They are living.
I am alive.   They are dead.
I am dead.   They are dead.
I am dead.   They are dead.
I am dead.   They are dead.
I am dead.   They are dead.

The Vapor

Events wound down to chaos.
Wanting to leave some trace,
Dietrich Bonhoeffer wrote his name
in his copy of Plutarch.
That book finds its way home,
his own life glowing from the Nazi dark.

When we touch the book of such a man,
when we hear his hymn
"O faithful God prepare my grave,"
or his last spoken words, "This is the end,
but now I begin to live,"
we breathe the erika vapor of those dead

who may come to comfort, and to bless
when next the runic lightning SS
slashes down. He tells us God is helpless
here in the world unless we share
His suffering, and thereby raise
all grief to holiness, to praise.

The murdered German pastor
who would have killed the Fuehrer
still sends us letters from his cell.
Sometimes, all God's prison bulbs go black.
Dietrich mists and wipes his glasses, sits back,
remembers a word that lights another candle.

The Children

I do not think we can save them.
I remember, within my dream, repeating
I do not think we can save them.
But our cars follow one another
over the cobblestones. Our dim
headlamps, yellow in fog, brush past,
at the center of a market square,
its cathedral's great arched doors.
I know, now, this is a city
in Germany, two years
after the Crystal Night. I think ahead

to the hospital, the children.
I do not think we can save them.

Inside this dream,
in a crystal dashboard vase,
one long-stemmed rose unfolds
strata of soft red light.
Its petals fall, tears, small
flames. I cup my palm to hold them,
and my palm fills to its brim,
will overflow.
Is this the secret, then? . . .
Now I must spill the petal light, and drive.

We are here, in front of the hospital,
our engines murmuring. Inside,
I carry a child under each arm,
down stairs, out to my car.
One's right eyeball hangs on its cheek
on threads of nerve and tendon,
but he still smiles, and I love him.
The other has lost her chin —
I can see straight down her throat
to where her heart beats
black-red, black-red.
I do not think we can save them.

I am the last driver in this procession.
Many children huddle in my car.
We have left the city. Our lights
tunnel the fog beneath arches of linden,
toward Bremerhaven, toward
the western shore.
I do not think we can save them.
This time, at the thought, lights
whirl in my mirror, intense
fear, and the screams of sirens.
I begin to cry, for myself, for the children.
A voice in my dream says
this was the midnight you were born. . . .

Later, something brutal happened, of course,
but as to this life I had to, I woke,
and cannot, or will not, remember.
But the children, of course, were murdered,

their graves lost, their names lost,
even those two faces lost to me. Still,
this morning, inside the engine of my body,
for once, as I wept and breathed deep,
relief, waves of relief, as though the dreamed rose

would spill its petals forever.
I prayed thanks. For one night, at least,
I tried to save the children,
to keep them safe in my own body,
and knew I would again. Amen.

This Night

Which is our star this night?
Belsen is bathed in blue,
every footworn lane, every
strand of wire, pale blue.
The guards' bodies,
the prisoners' bodies — all
black and invisible. Only
their pale blue eyes
float above the lanes
or between the wires.
Or they are all dead,
and these are the blue eyes of those
haunted by what happened here.
Which eyes are yours,
which mine? Even
blue-eyed crows
drift the darkness overhead. Even
blue-eyed worms
sip dew from the weeping leaves
of the black erika
over the graves. . . .
But now, at once, every
eye, every blue light
closes. As we do.
For rest. For now.
Which was our star this night?

The Chestnut Rain

(1986)

the infinite dead (the land entire saturated, perfumed with their
impalpable ashes' exhalation in Nature's chemistry distilled, and
shall be so forever, in every future grain of wheat and ear of corn,
and every flower that grows, and every breath we draw —
—Walt Whitman
Specimen Days

Sports and gallantries, the stage, the arts, the antics of dancers,
The exuberant voices of music,
Have charm for children but lack nobility; it is bitter earnestness
That makes beauty; the mind
Knows, grown adult.

— Robinson Jeffers
"Boats in a Fog"

The Snow Hen

1. (The Deer)

The first time there,
though I was just a boy,
I had been there before,
past, I remember, a ridge of stones
back of a field, and past a stand of pines
to Wenzel's furthest field

where one weeping,
blight-struck tree,
held center. . . .

A deer came toward me,
slowly, from groves far away,
stood near me,
dropping her head
from side to side,
her long lashes
bending up from wet chestnut eyes.

We were so quiet,
I could hear her heart.

I circled her neck,
buried my hands in her fur.
These were the same rhythms that held her. . . .

We stood there under a dome, under its center,
until gray dusk and a scatter
of early stars.
The last light shone from within her.
Now, here, evening unending
receives her,
holds us together, for one reason,
in the chestnut rain.

May that other world's light
circle around her, within her, again.

2. (The Chestnut Rain)

My parents had not been born,
and I am thirty-five
in bicentennial autumn as I begin (maybe
never to end)
this relation,
when the last wagons of families
pulled away
from the century's turn
into branch-arched
country lanes
to gather the chestnut rain.

Now we read of this,
of the hundred-foot tree that once, in airy-
white blossom or heavy
with pods of food,
distilled the American earth for us.
At Mount Vernon,
the Washingtons' roast wild turkey
was sewn stuffed with chestnuts.
Cattle and deer fattened
or held to life on the winter meat of chestnuts.
Now one book of trees says
"only a few scattered
sucker growths remain."

Nothing to replace it, maybe
never again:
that fruit
a brown dimension
like nothing else in nature;
when newly fallen,
of such a swirled,
teardropped shine
that even our children's eyes
seemed made
with less skill.

3. (The Soldier)

Last night, in dream, I found
the broken ribcage of a fawn,
* moss-green, twined*
*   with bindweed vines.*

> "Do you remember, Amy," her husband asked,
> "that one huge hollow trunk,
> our base for hide-and-seek, the one
> we sheltered in that day of sudden rain?"

Nearby, a buck, its branches
lit gold in evening air, rose
* from solid ground,*
*   and then a doe.*

> She nodded, blushed, and then
> this eighty-year-old woman told me how
> when she was a girl she played
> in thin woods behind her father's fields
> among the massive, fallen
> bodies of chestnuts.

They disappeared,
but this was all in shadow,
* chestnut shadow,*
*   one tree towering over the field.*

> "Some trunks were so big," she said,
> "I couldn't climb over, and I remember
> we often imagined them as soldiers
> lost in the Great War.

Part of the deepening air, I
touched that chestnut's trunk,
* its blight scars and war scars now healed*
*   in jagged miracles*

of new cambium and bark
the shapes of the future's lightning,
* flashes of meaning*
*   under my breastbone.*

Dreamer, old woman, old man,
I have curled up
in chestnut shadow
inside this hollow
soldier beside you.

Listen: his trunk curves
rain around us. Now,
from the soldier's shadow,
from the curved rain's source,
a light, a soft light:

from the tree's center, from the beginning,
from leaves glistening at summer's pitch,
a light, unfolding, a veincage of light.

4. (Stereoscope)

Always again, as it must, this double vision
becoming one: children
playing in the dead groves;

and this one: soldiers who died
in Whitman's arms, the sap
of his songs, the blood;

and this one: those whose faces the land
furrowed, who learned
to live with the land, to love.

5. (Disco)

In fly-specked white-gold bulb- and straw-light,
ammonia fume, vapor rising from manure,
cows low their natural music.

The same barn's hand-hewn chestnut beams arch above me.
Outside the morning's door,

I work a pump whose long stem sucks back the pollen-
flecked rain, and drink.

Will it happen, again? Now,
under elms back of the east pasture,
a farmer's body rises with the sun, . . .

but it's no use. I awaken,
and they are gone now, moved, retired,
dead with their asphalt farms,

their children and children's children
stepping from city curbs, swaying
on straps in subways, selling

fashions or gourmet fads in shops built on land where
their parents, and theirs, and theirs brought forth food.
They are gone now,

their homes torn down, or falling, abandoned,
their barns' weathered woods countryfying

walls of city or suburban bars called MacDonald's Farm,
or The Dairy, or The Homestead, where
all the lost children strain to sing,

or, in groundless disorienting strobe-
light and glitter, dance on plastic floors,
batteries in their heels, smoothing

their pampered blown-dry hair with hands
that never held a hoe, blinking catatonic eyes
that never watered a bed of loam with tears of thanks.

6. (The Snow Hen)

I once carried a pail of warm milk through falling snow
to Mrs. Wenzel in her kitchen,
sipped its sweetness

from a tin ladle, and knew, somehow, that something
important had happened,
and would.

I kept seeing the vapor cloud forming and rising
from the pail into the gentle flakes.
That same evening,

after feeding their new machine, placing the day's eggs
into circling chamois cups,
hearing them tumble

through their wash and rinsing, holding my hand
at the bottom of an incline
to receive them,

after drying each egg with a soft cloth, I began
to candle. We soon heard Wenzel
in the outer hall,

stomping snow from his boots.
Then he was behind me,
watching me turn

a perfect egg over the hole in the candling box,
translucence glowing from its oval soul,
not a single blood spot

within its finger-
shadowed
shell.

Wenzel, as he often did, made magic, pulled an egg
out of his Adam's apple
under his beard.

He'd found it in the snow, he said,
gift of the snow hen.
This one,

when I balanced it over the same upwelling light,
floated webs of the frailest bones,
patterns of frost

feathers, curves of white muscles,
and two spots, rice-
grains

of the chick's beginning eyes,
this whole world
revolving

as I turned the egg, or holding
still as I stared,
as I did,

as I do, both Wenzels watching as I evening-
dream my way again into this cosmos
of milk vapor and snow.

7. (The Light)

Be with me in the light of this prism,
for this is our earthly body again,
solar light broken down,
rays of decomposition,

black, white-banded lines of the chestnut's possible resurrection,

light of the house sparrow's chestnut nape, light

of a child you love, its first six lunar months within its mother
when cells move from matrix into cerebral cortex,

light filling your palms' valleys, now, if you'll open them,

which is, at last, the easeful light of your loins
and behind your eyes as you give yourself, man or woman,
to the flow of words, or semen,

light of the smallest atomic particle struck until split
into particles its own size, miracle
of the undiminished lord, light

of the ocean nautilus swaying, its empty innermost chambers
coiling back to their beginning,

light of the crystal lattice, light rising into grass at Arlington,

light of arctic night under the sliding pearl shelves,

light left in a dead human eye, curving outward,

light of trains rocking the last chestnut ties,

light of a new net strung on a rim mounted in a city alley,

light bursting upward with sidewalk pigeons,
the full spectrum of their circling above the buildings,

which is the light of which our daily light is shadow,

red light that enters arterial blood,

light of Mourningcloak larvae that once fed on elm leaves,

which is the honey-grained light of a chestnut cupboard,

light of half-moons drifting your father's nails,

which is the light of goldenrod shade,

light in spaces under snow-buried spruce boughs,

which is the light of the abandoned farm, light
of scattered boards, of sheds sagging into lilacs and sumacs,

candled light, blood spots balanced in the cosmos,

which is the light of the black-capped chickadee's ministry,

the milky light of a foal inside its mother above their meadow,

light entering our third eye,

light of the Buddha's ear, of Francis's tongue-tip tuned to beasts,

which is the light of palm kelp rooted in rock, springing back
against breakers until the simple light of Walt's *Leaves* unfolds,

but now ripped loose into the light of Landsberg and *Mein Kampf*,

aberrant light of killers working together,

intricate black revolving light of the Holocaust,

light shining from the last Bronx synagogue,

light that shadows every Jew, the light of Belsen *heide*,

which is the spectral light of old Salem's invisible wonders,

which is the light of chestnut rain, blossoms falling,
nuts ripening in falling burs,
rain that reached those branches, rain of light
through the toothed and thick-veined leaves,

which is the light seeping from atomic waste into our future,

light of dead snappers in dioxin swamps,

light of a pipeline burst above tundra,

light in the eyes of the last passenger pigeon,
campfire light of "Kansas oak" on the treeless plains,

light filling skin flaps over tepee openings, all facing east,

which is the light of Wyoming museum display cases holding
Chief Joseph's ax, Yellow Hand's scalp-knot,

which is the light of an Indian mummy curled in his grave,
string of bear-claw light still circling his neck,

the dusky light painted by Albert Bierstadt
on the flanks of the last buffalo
winding away from their hunters,

which is the light of the cruise missile named *Tomahawk*,

which is the light of buffalo oil burning in a clay dish,

the "clear, certain and perfect light" of Jonathan Edwards,

but drunken light skidding the human family tree,

which is the light of leukemia water,

but light traced in the wood of Jefferson's desk,

which is the light of William Schroeder's mechanical heart
which he described as a "threshing machine,"

but the slow sludge of poison light sliding into ocean trenches,

but the "quiet light" of Bryant's fringed gentian,

which is the light of the one smiling commuter in the packed car,
standing, swaying, reading the *Ramayana*,

which is the light of the Platte at Red Buttes on the Oregon Trail
where the river bends, where Robert Stuart camped in 1812
in the light of cottonwoods still growing
at the bend of the Platte under the red hills,

the transient, imploded, almost-remembered light
of the bare chestnut at evening in winter,

light of bottles buried back of our farms for hundreds of years,
blue of medicine, green of whiskey, amber of bitters,
the bubbled translucence of mineral-water flasks,

which is the light of the dead in the battle of Long Island in
the shadow of the church at Shiloh along
the Marne at Chateau-Thierry under
the Okinawa sand in the Mekong Delta's mud endless
American rollcall of corpselight,

which is the light of Fredericksburg,
meadowlarks lifting into sulphurous air,
settling again between the lines that trapped them,

light of oil still rainbowing above the *Arizona* at Pearl Harbor,

light falling into apple trees' opened heads,

which is the spiral light of the slave's hovel,

light of John Woolman's undyed clothes and journal,
light of his mind "frequently clothed with inward prayer,"

which is the light of the chestnut tamkin in the cannon's mouth,

rhapsodic light woven by earthworms in coffins,

which is the light of Alamogordo,
the never-ending radiostrontium of a mother's milk,

jugular light of our sunset rivers,

light of radium children,

which is the light of the dissolving chain, entropic light
crawling from dawn along its own curled tail,

which is the light lost to this earth forever,
light of an aborted child,

these lines at least the loosened black light of plowing,

light of the last holy chestnut leaves unfolding,

edge of eternal light scything out from a dead star,

light of ponds dusted with the last chestnut pollen,

which is the light inside the tears filling our closed eyes
    as we praise, and grieve.

The Ewe's Song

8. (Heartwood)

Darker,

but light's
blossom redolence
insists again,

a shutter,
an odor,
flash of picture:

doing no harm,
I repeat this dream,
descend, strip
the rough, fist-
deep bark
from a centuries-
old chestnut.

One by one, its
layers of living wood
peel away,
its trunk a blight-
scarred bell
of yellow skins.

I hear
the years' sounds
enter their own
wavery rings,
and water rising
into the breathing
cells of the chestnut's
body.
Be with me,

touch your tongue
to chestnut
wetness,
this taste
distilled of decades,
bittersweet
remembrance.

Soon,
eighty, ninety years
nearer the center
of our country,
we press
the heartwood
tinged
almost the black red
of dried blood,

until we hear
services in the air,
confusion

of running soldiers,
the circling camps
of Howe's battle hymn,
crackle of pitch-pine
torchlight,
women praying,
whispering at last,
at last, and crying.
Essence
of lilacs dead
a hundred years, until,

skin after skin,

the tree dying
into time again, we
awaken, knowing, somehow,
the fragrances
and sounds held
in the dreamed body
of a witness tree,
the enduring
taste of chestnut's
heartwood,
and the death of Lincoln.

9.   (At West Hills, Long Island)

As we stand in the room where Walt was born,
      fourth-month shadows pass through these windows
         with traces of his true body.
      As we close our eyes to the hearth's chestnut mantle

         (and enter the float forever
            held in suspension in eastern
               marsh grass and western redwoods in rivers
            that image our souls in fields where soldiers

return to their land in barn-chapels'
   haydust rays in hymns preserved
      in grains of pews in light diffused
   in rings of chestnut rain), we

awaken, breathing birth odors, the broken
   mother-water, placenta and blood that follow him
from his Island mother's womb,
   Island child, child of the world, until,

here in the scents and shadows of spring,
   surrounding lilacs assume that light again,
   light of this borning room, ever-
returning, streaming, and staying.

10. (Neighbors)

In 1897, his 78th year, a farmer
remembered that even during the war
steamers carried barrels of plums to New York City
from the whole Hudson River Valley.

You'd buy a smoked pigeon for a penny,
a handful of plums for another,
and walk while eating, tasting
the whole country on your tongue.

But the carts of pigeons emptied,
and the barrels of plums disappeared,
the valley's million trees lost
to wart-like excrescences, first thought

the onslaught of a new gall insect,
but, in fact, a parasitic fungus spread
by its own spores, even in mid-winter.
The only discovered cure was neighbors together,

and fire, amputating every black-knotted limb,
and fire, or summer color could not blossom,
again, as it did, from the ravaged plum.

11. (The Amber)

A certain sugar maple is dead,
chainsawed into sections, one bearing
   marks of more than a century of tapping
     that annual blessing, the spring flow.

It stood two hundred years between house and barn.
Our speech entered its living cells,
   and was preserved, as though in amber,
     as the tree grew. This is the tapped section now

   giving back its music, words rising from soil
into our parents' lungs (*oilmeal, planker*),
   when they were children, when, in old age,
     they rocked under the tree, speaking

   that language now for us of tongues
(*scours, wireworms, thrips, chalazae*),
   the sap now flowing from each wedge tapping
     the felled tree, for us to feel our lives again,

   to know with our whole bodies
(*Cobbler and Peachblow, bloodmash, Auroras*),
   out of the years, out of the dead tree
     (*curculio, mapleburn, widow's wheat, grapetear*) . . .

12. (The Ewe's Song)

Wenzel said "Come," and I followed him
through the gate into his farm.
We stooped beneath appletrees beginning to bud,
walked past the earth drenched black and red
under crossbars where he cut his chickens' throats.
In the back pasture, in the shed we entered,
its mother beside it softly bleating,
lay a spring lamb,
but the ewe's song was the saddest ever sung.

There, in the golden gloom of straw,
I saw her sadness: her lamb,
still half-sheathed in her placenta,
had only half become her lamb —
its forelegs and chest missing,

its forehead open to blue ridges of brain.
Here, walk with me again into the ewe's swelling song,
the buzz of stillness, the milky placenta,
into the dead lamb's glazed eyes.

Wenzel said "Come," and I followed him
through the gates of my childhood,
where he is buried now, alive.
The same stars still dome his acres,
now arranged with tracts of houses
whose dreamers sometimes awaken
smelling air of vanished coops, spring
appletrees and pastures, sheep sheds, feeling,
almost knowing they've heard the ewe's song.

13.   (The Dead)

I am in a dream, in that barn again.
Between stalls, squares of pale light sift snow.
In each stall, a deer.

Vapor lifts from their bodies
up to chestnut beams under the haymow.
I hear an engine whine, or my own electric brain.

Snow thickens in windows,
but now, somehow, the whole barn rises into white air
above the farm,

and I am on a train, with others,
who talk low, in plainsong,
as I knew they would.

They breathe vapor, fold
fur arms across their chests, and stare, straight ahead,
as I knew they would.

My window streams with night, and stars. Somewhere
an engine winds down, as the dead around me
brighten, and fade.

14. (The Steer)

I saw a farmer's eyes fill with the light
of a story that began *so help me*:
he said he'd once had a steer that cared for flowers,
not as food, but cared as we do.
Light gray, almost silver, beautiful animal itself
within the herd, it spent hours carrying the season
of bluets, asters, bindweed blooms
in its mouth from one side of its pasture to the other.
Before it browsed on grass, it laid down its flowers.
Finished, it picked them up again,
and carried them about again, as though
it had a soul, so help him.

That farmer is dead, his pasture paved,
his soulful story lost, except for here.
When you see the silver-gray steer,
you are in the farmer's eyes,
you are his light, *so help me*.

15. (Foals)

Top of her buttocks
    back of her hips,

her muscles have melted away.
    Now wax appears

on the brood mare's teats:
    in three days she will foal.

(Be with me here to witness,
    but quiet, out of her sight, and time.)

            She lies on her side, and widens.
                Her young one's

            wet fore-feet
                reach the stall's mellow light first,

            and then its nose, and then, quickly,
                its whole body slides forth wrapped

            in folds of opalescent placenta,
                which she nips away.

Exhausted, she tongues
her foal's whole body,

and nudges him, within an hour,
to her teats' thick yellow fore-milk,

colustrum, which must cleanse him.
This time,

yes, a male, and strong,
but the farm's seasons circle until

a just-delivered foal, a female,
lies still,

cannot breathe, the mare confused.
We'll cradle this foal in our arms, blow hard

up its muzzle and into its mouth.
We'll rub her damp body until

her first slow breath, feed her
a few spoonsful of brandy and water,

and if her dam will not regard her,
sprinkle flour over the newborn's back,

until this draws her mother to her,
or, if her mother still ignores her,

you and I, together,
will dry the foal with flannel,

will help her find the mare's teats,
and press her lips, until she tastes.

16. (Brahma)

This is the power of seed and humus.
This heals abscess, draining pus.

This heaps baskets with blackberry light.
This turns young sunflowers back at night.

This is the film always exposing
to marigolds flashing at evening.
This is the force that loses nothing.

Keeping, passing, turning again,
this is the chestnut rain.

This is the flux of spore and vapor.
This is the part that captures the actor.
These are the lovers abjuring their censor.

17. (This Woman)

   Outside our window,
rain falls
      through leaves
     themselves falling
through the rain.

                Will this be broken?

   I lie on my left side,
she on her right.
     This woman still loves me,
   has given us children,
wants me to speak again.

                Will this be whole?

   She moves to me in bed,
cups my testicles in her fingers and palms,
     traces the raised veins of my penis,
   still small, but now
beginning to swell,

   in a few minutes the length
of one of her hands from wrist
     to end of center finger.
   She presses
my heart-shaped tip

   with the fingers of her right hand,
rolls my shaft
     in her loose left fist,
   her woman's grip small,
but able to circle and fulfill. . . .

She feels my breath in her hair,
curves lower,
        now holds me with both hands
    and in the space
between her teeth and lips.

    For me, for her,
this is a ring
            of warm light,
    light that will hold,
will widen.

                        Will this be broken?
                        Will this be whole? . . .

    She does not always want this,
but wants it now,
        tastes my first thin fluid on her tongue,
    feels her eyes roll
under her closed lids.

        She cradles my sac in her right hand,
holds my moist shaft
        still in the circle of her left,
    tongues and sucks me
to her own rhythms,

    as these become mine, as these become yours.
My hands pass through her hair,
        cup her ear,
    now a shell filled with only
the surf of our bodies.

    Moving her head slowly,
she feels the final swell,
        knows the surf must poise,
    constrict, break,
and flow.

                    Now. . . .

    She swallows once,
again. My hand falls from her ear.
        I touch her tongue, throb smaller.
        Gently, she will sip me, until I'm empty,
until another time. You understand. . . .

Sounds of the leaves
begin again.
    This will be whole.
   She can still
taste my semen,

   feel tendrils of its light
behind her closed eyes,
      on her tongue,
  in her lungs as she breathes,
and here. . . .

      I have drifted, crested,
am drifting back again
     into her body,
  drifting back,
into her body. . . .

18. (This Blossom)

Sleepers, soldiers, farmers, lovers —
what is their connection?
Can it be any clearer?
What is the chestnut rain?

Once, in a field, a doe came toward me,
stood near me, has not left,
lives within this living tree
if you will hear her heart.

We'll wait near this trunk a while
while light curves back again
filled with the words of hymnals,
matters of brain and breastbone,

even hum the childhood melody
of bellows and sinewy hands
under the spreading tree
where the village blacksmith stands.

We'll kneel for those who cannot hear him,
lie down with those who can,
and rest, within this eighteenth blossom
of the chestnut rain.

Blackberry Light

19. (Praise)

Such long silence? How much time is by?
I fell away, disbelieved,
returned like a dog to my
own vomit, as Edwards testified.

Do I wish to awaken?
Are these questions my awakening?
Let it happen, then, again,
this dreamed tree rising

in communion, its trunk
branchless for twenty feet.
This is the stripped bark:
take, eat;

this the body to break,
chew, swallow.
Knees, bend. Neck,
bow. Know

wholeness. Lips, kiss
whatever made the chestnut rain —
God of dung and broken stone,
incarnate darkness,

God toward which the chestnut's eyes
have always turned, tree
waiting like thick honey
under infected skies,

God of the dead-haunted heart,
praise, if we can, praise,
if we should, in blight-struck wood,
this time in your own coin, praise.

20. (The Wind)

Now the wind, once given words by branches and leaves,
our own words for us to hear, to have,
and those other words from Venus and our graves,
moves more quietly past Chestnut Ridge,
over Chestnut Hill, through Chestnut Lane,
moaning, if anything, of something missing,
but bearing nevertheless the rain.

21. (The Tie)

"Note old chestnut tie in foregound,"
the caption says. This photograph, in black and white,
in a railroad bulletin,
holds the old bed, overgrown, looking west,
of the New York & Pennsylvania line
somewhere in winter in an ash wood.
Our view is an intrusion,
so quiet is the snow-dusted glade.

Above the tie and past it, and in this section spoken,
when not to you, to no one, what could have been
rails' vanishing point is hidden in limbs.
Only the one visible tie, in all this stillness, hums,
but when we stare for a long time,
we stand in center picture as the last train
pulls away, saplings appearing within our hearing
behind it. . . . The tie, of course,

in this photographic meditation —
note the way it sheds snow, note
pith-rot shadows rising from inside it —
remembers nothing, not the rain of its own leaves,
not one soldier, not even the last caboose passing
into the light of dead time above it.
But we do, even as we remember nothing,
as we stare, as we may or may not want to.

22. (The Bodies)

Inside, we light candles, and wait.
As we find our seats,
the last gates clang shut.

Will we ever pass our evenings in the old way,
watching moths blur the streetlamps,
breathing the chestnuts' infinite shades of green?

Now, the President's voice:
Our wars are almost over.
We repeat, almost over, almost . . .

Below us, wrapped in flags,
small loaves in the darkness. . . .
The stadium's dome begins to glow.

Soon, we'll line up.
We'll pass through turnstiles, file onto the field,
circle the bodies with candles.

Each spring each body will break
into radium blossoms we'll buy
from our soldiers, particles

of chestnut light in our bloodstreams, seen
from the next passing star.

23. (The Cross Section)

A tilt-stand schoolroom magnifier,
and this disk, this cross section,

its growth arranged in circles, yes,
but life's disorderly burstings, insect pits,

pores where sap pooled, verticle resin ducts,
outlets to the porous bark, the air. . . .

Move the section slowly,
travel its hues from blood to honey. . . .

Twenty-third from the center, there,
a ring that frost shaped, stained,

seeped into, now seeming like rust held
in memory by the tree. But cells kept

   bubbling outward, for weather could wound
     but not stop up that life upwelling

      as the tree filled with buds,
        with bees dusted with pollen, not do

         what blight did decades later
          to the last two, or three,

            or four layers of formless wood.

24. (Blackberry Light)

Old man Wenzel, try to forget the yellow manure
   seeping from under your sick ewes,
     the mucus and cheesy matter
coughed up by tuberculer cows,

exhaustion of plantings four times washed lost or blown lost,
   your Mrs. weeping softly
     all the way to sleep,

rats to drown from their tunnels under the hen roosts,
   blood-fat tics to singe from the dogs,
     wood to split and carry, garbage to bury
back of the fields behind the lordly maples,

bushels of dead chicks when your stove failed them,
   the ears of your rabbits infested with maggots,
     the eyes of your sheep struck blind by your sledge,

and the vapor of birth smells, the tastes
   of your own slaughtered lambs,
     the hayloft's only window where you sometimes sat alone,
light streaming in past cobwebs hooked with flies. . . .

Old man Wenzel, try to forget the parting loam,
   the spring morning's sun illumining
     your hunched-over, pale-green cotyledons,

and when, after rain, you leaned into dripping leaves,
   filled your palm with blackberries, and ate them,
     your whole farm vanishing for moments
of blackberry light behind your eyes,

the almost invisible, silvery tent-worms' rails
   along the apple limbs, those tiny lives,
      before you burned them, each evening returning

from branched world to central cocoon,
   their frail and perishable home.

25. (The Butter)

This is the separator, working by gravity,
   milk kept cool in it for two days, and now
      skimmed with a shallow sterile ladle.

      Not musty, now ready, filled with limewater
   over the long winter,
this is the wood churn, best for butter,

which will not stick to it.
   This is the sweetest cream,
      with which Wenzel will fill it,

      pouring through the mesh
   of a copper wire strainer.
This is the medium-speed churning,

the attendant pleasant muscle-
   ache and dreaming,
      for a half-hour to an hour,

      remembering snow and the winter table,
   until the cream loosens
on the churn's sight glass:

the butter is forming.
   A little while longer, a few revolutions more,
      and this is the opening,

      and the washing-out of the butter-
   laden churn with fresh milk,
and the easy working of the paddles,

two or three turns through the butter,
   and the pouring-off of the milk again,
      until, over the butter still in the churn,

this is the sprinkling of salt to taste,
  and the waxy, compact butter
he'll press into a stone jar,

and this is the stone jar, covered
  with a boiled cloth and the jar's
    heavy lid,

    and this is the waiting jar
  of salted sweet-cream butter
stored down-cellar for the coming winter.

26.   (Images and Shadows)

Images and shadows of divine things —
what is the chestnut, then, where is its Lord?

If we could see,
we could see it whole,

not as root, trunk, light-drinking leaf,
thorned bur, but whole,

this history of time,
waves of spore and fungus,

the chestnut sipped dead, but shoots suffering
the viral light again, but saplings dying,

but new shoots straining upward, but dying,
but poking from root-source into air again, until,

in the end, the chestnut is sibilance,
our lips forming its sounds,

and the murmuring of *r*, and the *d*
of *wood*, and *dead*, the vowels

born within when our bodies
first felt the world want more than silent meaning,

if we could see its soul,
the whole tree candled,

if we could see,
if we could see it whole.

27. (The Poem)

Since the outbreak of the present war,
immense quantities of vegetables evaporated
in the kiln plants of western New York State
. . . have been shipped to France and
England as an army ration.
— E.L. Kirkpatrick (1918)

These are not watercolors of old farmhouses, their dooryards
     awash in hollyhock light,
          not little white churches in the valleys, their steeples
ringed with storybook clouds. . . .

These are not golden wedding couples in their buggies,
     haloes of bluebirds painted above them,
          not village ice-cream parlors where the young folks meet,
oh so shyly, blushing over their cherry phosphates,

not ballads of boys in torn breeches, their feet dangling
     over wooden bridges, their bobbers rippling,
          not their sisters in school learning to write, sweetly,
in feminine hand, feathery. . . .

These are not Main Street elms in nineteenth-century moonlight,
     or Chestnut Lanes where gaslamps glow upward
          to the undersides of leaves and send leaf-shadows
sailing to the stars, . . .

but these are not the aesthetics
 of carcinoma, planes flying
  defoliant cancer missions,
   cornfields controlled by computers,
    adulterated foods tasting
     like element charts, corporate
      swaddling-clothes-to-shroud
       packaging of people, sowlots
        solidified to shopping malls,
         antelope crucified
          on steel rods anchored
          in concrete, coal
         sludge meadows, chemical
        cattle, symmetrical
       watersheds, forced breast-
      and crotch-bulge
     advertised and worshiped, silt
    reservoirs, the last thistledown
drifting against a power line, . . .

but these are soldiers returned
        to their land, listening
    to grapevines humming the hard words
of grace at evening,

cycles of children burying
        parents in rain
    blinding with tears,
with blessing,

sheep shorn of moonlight
        by arthritic hands,
    grain that seeds
as it is eaten. . . .

These are the future cities'
        talismanic flails
    riveted to their walls,
the astral blood received

of the lambs' tails severed
        on Wenzel's kitchen table,
    these the tail stumps, ikons
swabbed with iodine. . . .

These are memorial cells
        of passenger pigeon
    in every bushel of garden dirt
or diesel air,

slices of harvest
        drying in trays still set
    on registers in chestnut floors,
or on stoves

in autumn homes lit
        with the mystical fruit
    and vegetable flesh
of the land, and the dead.

28. (The Girl)

It was autumn when Li Po heard a girl picking chestnuts
by the shore humming, "Evening now,
I must be home."

His poem ends there . . . but the girl reached home, and that night
dreamed of walking the shore again
where the chestnut wood

gave her our song. Inside each chestnut, she knew,
was night — each was an eye
in her fingers,

and she, as she slept, could see, with those chestnut eyes,
rain in the dying trees a thousand years away,
the trees, too, on their way home

in a beam of light, in a curve of time to where
we and Li Po's girl resume
that autumn dream.

29. (Auction)

Late, I was in the back circle.
    Just out of beginning rain,
        the auctioneer stood on a wagon

pulled to the central doors of a sagging barn,
    and sold — rolls of barbed wire, tools, feed,
        furniture, depression glassware, a mirror,

linens, a shotgun, Christmas decorations —
    all held up by his young helpers.
        Then, a box of books. I bid a dollar,

and they were mine, passed back
    by a dozen hands. I knelt to sort them,
        knowing what they'd be, as they were —

those same popular weeping novels
    of the century before: a woman, of course,
        who stands in her doorway wondering whether

to wed her city or her country suitor; a priest,
    of course, who loves the village's spinster teacher
        for sixty years of heartbreak without a word. . . .

You know what I mean — the language-cloying
    conventional sublime
        that dazes and bores us. But there, too,

in the bottom of the box, a scrapbook,
   and pasted on its first yellowed and chipped page,
      a photograph of the girl who'd kept it

seventy years before, who'd pressed into it
   and labeled leaves she'd known,
      oak and maple, apple, linden,

black birch, catalpa, and then, still green
   in folds of waxed paper, "American Chestnut,"
      these leaves bought at auction

in arrogance in the gentle rain, but now down
   on my knees, eyes blurred in the light of dead trees
      and the face of a girl who gathers

the farm's beauty in fallen leaves,
   who needed to touch, touched, still
      touches these pages of the chestnut rain.

30. (The Bark)

Now, alone, as my morning train rocks east
over Kansas plains, their wheat
blowing in gold waves in the sun,
time has come, again, somehow, to begin.

I cradle in my hands an oval of Pacific-
rounded bark I knelt for
while walking with a friend
at Seal Rock, on the Oregon coast. . . .

The fir bark, when I scrape my thumbnail
along its sides, gives of itself
fragrances of ocean kelp
and faint evergreen air, sends

intermittent mica signals, until, for the first time,
I see the almost transparent sandgrains
embedded in the bark's softer veins,
until, here in the train's rhythmic light,

I see myself a child again
walking dunes banking
the Atlantic shore, alone,
except for insects visible only

by their shadows. I remember kneeling
to a plant whose low glow
seemed to have lasted past death
in an iridescent paleness:

I broke its stem-stump,
pulled apart its ribbed jacket,
and saw, arranged in evenly spaced horizontals,
hundreds of plant jewels, sandgrains

drawn by the force that makes land,
lifted from chaos into ideas of forest,
held by the dead beach plant, the dusty miller,
for a boy to see, and remember,

pinweed, bayberry, sea rocket,
sparse in their dune deserts,
but all holding clumps of sand
out of the mindless drift and flow,

as here, this recurring gift, memory.
The mid-country light blurs. My train
hurtles, again, into the jeweled valleys
of my own bark body.

31. (The Tunnel)

Washed in light in tones of brown,
I am on a flatcar,
kneeling, parallel to a plain,
toward which, to my left, I turn. Someone shouts

"Look," and I do. There, in the distance,
parallel to my travel,
appear trunks of dead trees, some wrenched
on twisted crotches, some hunched

on limb elbows, but all
smooth, immense, unbelievable
in fallen grandeur,
backlit, but becoming clearer,

until someone whispers, "chestnuts,"
until I see, from even this far,
yellow blight scars blotting the huge forms,
as my train moves on,

past hundreds, until
I look into my own chest, seeing
the same yellow animal beating, knowing
that the flatcar I am riding is a dream of time

just after the chestnut rain. . . .

But now, haze,
   and the bare plain
      fades, almost lost,
         but begins again,

pulse beat, brain
   hymn, rocked
      ties, rail
         rhythm, memories

of trees once alive
   in the plain's light,
      in the distance,
         toward which I turn,

all this foreknown, in sepia,
   photograph I have seen,
      doubled, stereoscope card
         at an auction where the dead

farmer's fields reached
   unbroken to horizon,
      whose photograph blurred
         with unexpected tears,

all this known
   within this dream,
      understood,
         but just as I begin,

as the haze lifts,
   to fall away,
      awaken,
         I lift my eyes

higher on the plain,
   and see it, there,
      far past the known line
         where the others fell,

towering over
  the twig branches
    of the chestnuts:
      tree,

the world tree,
right-angle in visible cross-
section against the plain,
rain clouds passing the upper curves of its annual rings,

and nothing before imagined or seen
had brought me here
to the flatcar beating west above the plain, past
the fallen chestnuts to this trunk

of the first tree,
its interrupted rings around the clotted heartwood grown
when living time began,
nothing but witness power within,

and this itself born with the great tree,
as now the flatcar sings on rails
bending into the light
of that red-black heartwood tunnel,

and I know why I kneel.

32. (The Muse)

Don't turn to this so quickly. Go back, maybe
to where two girls assume our chestnut dream,
maybe to time's field, the deer and weeping tree. . . .

Only her hair tendrilling out into light on her pillow,
the muse of this poem now needs to rest in shadow.
We'll slow down, go back with Wenzel to his meadow.

She'll sleep, dreamless, or, as she turns her face to the moon,
may see and hear, but deeper, the music of chestnut rain,
all she has given and been. We'll leave her, for now,

to her lunar sleep, until she awakens to kiss us again.

Wenzel

33. (The Psalm)

Done for the long day,
dazed and pleasured in his bone-ache,
having earned his food again, stretched out flat on his back
in the near meadow, hands behind his head, eyes
closed as the last light

filters away,
Wenzel believes, says to himself
I have been here before, have always been here,
where we will place him in the grass
in increasing certainty,

will loose near him a ewe
to graze forever. Her nose nuzzles
each blade for a century, and each new shoot she nips short
grows back as she chews. Near her,
her lamb wobbles

into this evening
spring of the world, and its soft,
hopeful bleating, our psalm of time, somehow reminds him,
this memory so still for him for so long,
of when he was a child,

of farmhouse windows
flowing muffled voices of sheep,
as we overhear them now during the gathered moments:
ewe, lamb, dusk, farmer at rest, eyes
closed as last light

holds still
where we will leave him
as he breathes, *I have been here*
before, have always
been here.

34.   (Science Fiction)

Is it too late to save it, our first earth?
I shift Wenzel, again, to another world.
Chestnut rain is with him, but as spirit
held for now unfallen in the mind.

You know how he arrived: within
prophecy in fiction of man's desire,
the home planet ruined, the grass here
on his timeless farm bluer and faster-growing.

This is the world to which his dead sheep died,
and when he stares into their all-seeing eyes
where stars drift in depthless pupils,
he knows he's in my dream, nearer to Virgo,

and what I've done. For some reason, he says no,
but can't resist me. I give him
four or five moons in the day sky alone,
pastures, woods, orchards, wife,

children: at the thought, myself
a child again, I stand in that same field
where this began. That tree rises.
My doe appears in the chestnut rain.

35.   (That Socket)

Wenzel sucked a fresh egg through a pinhole.
    This makes life, he said, and handed me the shell.
        I fill that hollow oval world on paper.
I follow him from sleep, to shed, to stall.

Wenzel smeared his chest with wet manure.
    This makes life, he said, and breathed deep.
        That light here glistens in his chest hair.
I follow him from stall, to shed, to sleep.

Wenzel bit a hen in her red comb.
    This makes life, he said, and licked her head.
        I taste that blood in any lip or blossom.
I follow him from sleep, to stall, to shed.

Wenzel lost an eye to the plucking drum.
    This makes life, he said, and winked
        that socket of clotted blood. I follow him
across the darkening acres of his farm.

36. (The Whistle)

Along the edge of his furthest field,
Wenzel cut a section from a chestnut root
to make a whistle that he'd seen his father make.
When he blew it, the usually shy grackles and red-
winged blackbirds flew from far, fluttered
near him as he moved. Hundreds trailed him home,
waited all afternoon in backyard trees
to hear that sound again.

Could two species share the same flocking note?
Could they have heard a dying nestling? . . .
They seemed tranced, charmed, unafraid.
Was this the gene-trail music of migration
heard in the wind though chestnut wood
since the first blossoming? Whatever it was,
we'll leave them here, and listen: all evening,
Wenzel plays these simple sounds

fashioned from a chestnut root,
spells of the grackle, redwing, human heart.

37. (The Scrapple)

Wenzel brought in a blood-stained burlap ball,
    unwrapped a head, a hog's head, eyeless,
        already scalded hairless.

    Mrs. sawed it into quarters, removed
    brain, skin, ears, and snout,
sliced off the fattest parts for lard.

Mrs. soaked the lean remainder
    overnight in lemon juice and water
        to dissolve the gluey matter. . . .

Morning, she set this boiling, then
   picked out all bones, drained off
maybe half the liquor.

Mrs. stirred in corn meal, stirred it in thick,
   boiled the mixture for an hour, added
      salt and pepper, removed it from the fire,

      turned the scrapple into a shallow dish to mold,
   covered it with cloth until solid,
then served it thin-sliced and cold, or fried.

38.   (Family Tree)

Our children, and theirs,
and theirs out to the blight-struck
chestnut branches, feel
something missing, almost
past remembering, and now
putter in suburbs, swallow
the lives of pop stars,
repeat, over drinks, strained jokes
of farmers and drunks,
bore themselves in video oblivion,
collect antiques or primitive tools
to turn a profit, or hang
from subway straps, or buy and sell
sexless fashions, or jars of synthetic foods
in hyped and seasonless stores
built on land worked by those
whose names spill
from disbound bibles,
whose portraits weep from albums
sold by box lots at auctions, the faces
of those men and women who knew

how to handle a double-edged, curved-blade pruning saw,

how to cleft-, inlay- and whip-graft,

how to tell fruit-buds from leaf-buds,

how to help trees heal winter-split boles,

how to paddle berries from their bushes,

how to spring-trap a mole,

how to take a horse's pulse, how to pound out a shoe,
how to clean the cleft between sole and frog,

how to treat cabbage seed for black-rot,

how to use the sunshine tables when building a hog house,

how to insert the trocar and canula when treating hoven,
how to tie an animal's head to a stanchion for dehorning,

how to stun,

how to protect a new queen until she acquires the colony's odor,

how to douche the bull's sheathe,

how to write in blackberry light,

how to bore taproots for blasting stumps off below plow depth,

how and where to store seed ears,

how to measure femininity in the ewe,

how to treat an egg-bound hen,

how to rub caustic potash over horn lumps until they bleed,

   in the light of the fifth-of-an-inch chestnut puparium
      of the onion maggot

   in the light of a semi-hard strain of winter wheat called "Nigger"

   in the light of fields of purple and white loco

   in the light of Maine pines so immense that twenty yokes of oxen
      strained to haul one from forest to wharf

   in the light of rangeland dried up and blown away,
      of dust clouds where three-foot grasses once waved

   in the light of Kentucky humus washed into the sea

why crimson clover is the best winter cover,

why to scatter grass seed in light snow over the pasture,

why not to buy a boar with small testicles,

why to burn or bury the sow's afterbirth,

why to ring a hog's nose,

why cabbage seedlings sometimes take on a bluish cast,

why to keep light from stored dried vegetables and fruit,

why to sow buckwheat where subsoil is hard,

why to pin down the tips of the canes of drooping blackberry,

why to pare fruit with a silver knife, why to drop the fruit
  into cold water made acid with lemon juice,

why to prune the peach tree, but allow the cherry to assume
  its own shape,

why to keep the stallion colts from mares after one year,

why allow the newborn calf's navel blood to escape,

why some calves breathe, or gasp, only a few times, and die,

why to fear blueness in the nostrils of cattle,

why the skin on a hog's snout sometimes turns purple,

why a hog might kneel to stretch its throat along the ground,

why not to store manure under the eaves upon the steep hillside
  along the brook,

why a ram is half the flock,

why some chicks appear rumpled and act stupid,

why to raise their brooder above the floor,

why fowls sometimes pull out their own feathers,

why to make hens hunt their grain in deep straw,

why not to furnish deep straw for a litter of pigs,

why to fall plow, why not to fall plow,

why to cover alfalfa hay with canvas,

> *in the light of Texas stockmen whose "free grass for all"*
>   *would never run out*
>
> *in the light of Jacob Waltz's lost mine*
>
> *in the light of smudge pots smoking in the citrus groves*
>
> *in light held in the bodies of all those who tasted syrup*
>   *from maples tapped for two hundred years*

but they are gone now, dead with their asphalt farms,
their homes torn down, or falling, abandoned,
their neighbor-raised barns selling for wood wanted
to flavor the atmosphere in city bars
where lost children strain to sing,
or dens where bored suburbanites tune in
insipid midday pseudo-dramas while the sun
burns above a land once lived for by families who knew

when corn was in its milk stage, ready for drying,

when to take dewberries from drying tray or kiln,

when to scrape rough bark from old appletrees,

when and where to place the china eggs,

when to shallow- and when to deep-plow,

when to cut the millet,

when to loose ewes on luxuriant pasture,

when to turn and change positions of incubated eggs,

when and how long to cool them,

when to replace hen-roost bulbs with ruby-colored lights,

when to rely on sunlight, and when to disinfect,

when to feed pounded garlic to pheasants,

when to moisten a feather with turpentine or kerosene
    and insert it into a chick's throat,

when and where to set tomatoes out,

when bumblebees can pollinate and honeybees can't,

when to spray poison into the calyx cup,

when to use a bar shoe,

when to watch the middle horse of the three-horse team,

when accumulations of coagulated serum in gelatinous form
    clog an animal's body,

> in the light of Walt's gifts to soldiers: blackberries,
>   peaches, lemons and sugar, wines, preserves, pickles,
>   brandy, milk, tobacco, tea — "so I go round,—
>   some of my boys die, some get well —"

when bluing water is sufficiently blue,

when to apply grease, when to smear sheep's nostrils with tar,

when an afterbirth should drop away, and when, if it doesn't,
    to remove it, and how to,

when to castrate the male calves,

when to expect slightly bloody milk,

when blood oozes in drops from the thighs of sheep,

when cows freshen,

when never to drag a dead animal over the ground to its grave,

*in the light of Jefferson, who knew the psychic income
    from living under sycamores*

not to feed horses crimson clover that has ceased to flower,

in the light of Jim Bridger speaking a dozen Indian tongues

not to plant peach trees on the south slope,

*in the light of buffalo grass and curly mesquite
    at the mouth of the Brazos*

not to pasture sheep in moist alfalfa,

*in the light of five and a half billion board feet of timber
    pouring out of Michigan in 1889 along the Ontonagon,
    Paint, Iron, and Sturgeon rivers, the loggers by then
        planning to move west for shade*

not to hang a harness above manure,

*in the light of the 19th-century Pacific Coast's virgin forests
    of fir, redwood, white pine, the heaviest stands on earth
        all the way to that time of the world*

not to feed an animal a day and a half before its slaughter,

*in the light of that language now for us of tongues:
    swale hay, corm, tarry blood, ringbone, blackspot
        apple canker, cherry slug, brown rot to stone fruit,
            strawberry weevil, bitter wood, hen bloom, iris worm*

not to brood chickens for two years on the same ground,

in the light of the farmers Wenzel who knew

that on the seventh day, the egg's live germ, if strong,
    shows blood vessels branching in all directions,

that clover and rape are the best egg flavors,

that the laying-hen's vent is large, moist, crescent-shaped,

that her crop and gizzard are her hopper and millstone,

that skimmed milk best moistens her mash,

that lice will puncture her quills to get to her blood,

that owls will enter the open windows of a brooder,

that cold hens are never happy, and will not lay,

that hens need light and lime, and love meat,

that a hog-pastured orchard increases its yield,

that a single live dodder seed menaces the crop,

that healthy calves' preputial tuft hairs are white, clean,
    and separate,

that a ton of urine is worth more than a ton of dung,

that honeybees, in their habit of constancy, will not carry
    dandelion pollen to apple flowers,

that clouds keep bees near their hives,

that shears can crush, while a saw cuts horns clean,

that darkened stables draw fewer flies,

that wheat and rye thrash clean, while oats remain in hull,

that buzzards, crows, dogs spread cholera from herd to herd,

— *I know I'm a swivel-chair cowboy*
    I know the farm disappears from my own body
    I've built hog houses to stand north and south
    I've come to this country with syringe and chilled semen
    I drink from a cup marked "Chu Lai RVN"

I've cleared and plowed slopes too steep to hold soil

I've traced a bindweed root four feet down
  and poured salt into the hole

I've kept time to the music of the Swede fiddle —

that lamb-twinning is only ten percent inherited,

that medicine can't reach worms in a sheep's fourth stomach,

that cows have dewclaws,

that newborn pigs suckle every two hours during the day,

that the silked ear is female, the tassel and pollen male,

that grapevines bleed at spring pruning,

  in the light of spots of poppy-blood in remembered fields

that air drains frost from blossoming strawberry slopes,

  in the light of missiles in their prairie silos

that autumn frost deepens the flavor of kale,

  in the light of the squarish, fluted contours of blackberry canes

how to stretch and electrify a fence,

  in the light of cattle drooling anthrax

when to pour a cup of cream into boiling maple sap,

  in the light of trays of drying raspberries

how to compost,

  in the light of migrant laborers' work songs

  in the light of a chestnut that scented the air over a cabin at Walden

  in the light of the mountain fiddler's music called "Soldier's Joy."

39. (This River)

Autumn trees drowned in the light of what Walt called
"the prevailing cosmic color, yellow —
yellow, tinged with brown."

God rendered vastnesses between stars, among galaxies,
in this brown-tinged yellow.
The chestnut

washed by mountainsides into that cosmic light come for it
from where space itself curves
illogically back,

here, within remembrance, where everything once alive
fills with that color again.
The trees return

to further than the furthest star, as we await ourselves
in the same light that reaches there,
this river.

40. (The Wool)

Clean, bur-free, and all-of-a-piece,
or the wool is almost useless,
so Wenzel upends a sheep gently

onto washed floorboards,
kneels to it, knees it still,
careful to console it as he holds it.

I hear electric whirr under
the sheep's plaintive bleating,
Wenzel shearing first its rump, then

brisket and neck, down
shoulders to belly, smoothly, then
the left side and then the right. . . .

I lift this full fleece away,
this harvest without death,
the shorn sheep rising, returning

to fold, frightened, maybe chilled,
but closer to its inner light,
and no worse off for its gift.

41. (The Heart)

I saw Wenzel's left hand on the ram's poll, his right under its chin.

I heard Wenzel talk to me to tell me.

I saw him twist the ram's head sharply upward.

I heard the ram's neck snap, saw its legs jerk and quiver.

I saw Wenzel lay the ram on a platform, hang its head over the end.

I saw myself look up into the gray autumn sky.

I saw him grasp the ram's chin in his left hand and slip a knife
    through its neck just back of its jaw.

I heard the ram's one gurgled and choked cry. . . .

I saw Wenzel cut the ram's flesh toward the spinal column to bone.

I smelled Wenzel's sweat and the ram's blood.

I saw a pail fill with bright blood and the blood's vapor.

I saw him split the skin over the back of the front legs
    from dewclaws to above the knees.

I saw him open the skin over the windpipe from brisket to chin.

I saw him split the skin over the back of the hind legs,
    and skin the buttocks.

I saw him raise the skin over the cod and flanks.

I saw him skin around hocks and down to the ram's hoofs.

I saw him cut off the hind feet at the toe joints.

I saw him run his knife between the cords and bone
    in back of the shins.

I saw him tie the ram's hind legs together.

I saw him pulley the ram by its hind legs to an elm branch.

I saw him fist the pelt free, cutting it off close to the ram's ears.

I saw him cut off the ram's head.

I felt myself holding the weight of the ram's head in my arms.

I saw myself look upward from the ram's eyes. . . .

I saw Wenzel cut the ram's cod to its breastbone.

I saw him peel away the ram's paunch and intestines.

I saw him split the breastbone and hold the ram's heart.

I saw the heart lift away with lungs and diaphragm attached.

I saw him reach up into the ram's pelvis and remove its bladder.

I saw him wipe blood and dirt from the ram's body.

I saw him rest, his back against the elm, as the ram's body
   cooled behind him. . . .

I saw him lift the ram's carcass down and shoulder it to his barn.

I saw him split the ram in two with a hatchet.

I saw him cut off the flank and breast of each half, and each leg
   at the hip joint.

I saw him cut off the shoulders between third and fourth ribs.

I saw him sever neck halves from shoulders at the neck vein. . . .

I saw Wenzel again that night walking toward the living ram.

I saw the ram wait for him against the gray sky.

I saw the ram's heart through its wool.

I saw Wenzel reach into the ram's chest for its heart.

I saw the ram nuzzle Wenzel's left palm for grain
   as Wenzel reached with his right hand for its heart.

I saw Wenzel's hand pass though the ram's ribcage.

I saw Wenzel holding its heart as the ram faded from view. . . .

I saw myself pass through the wall of a shed in Wenzel's field.

I saw a just-born lamb smoking in its damp wool in a bed of
   straw.

I smelled the ewe's water, saw her pale-blue placenta in the
   straw.

I saw two baby hearts beating in the lamb's chest.

I heard the lamb calling to Wenzel to take its second heart.

I heard Wenzel call to me to tell me.

I saw myself step into Wenzel's shadow.

I saw Wenzel's shadow enter the shed where the lamb sang. . . .

42. (The Leaves)

My friend has sent me two chestnut leaves
from a New Hampshire hillside.
They still hold the green fragrance of graves
near where sucker-growth sprouted,
once more, this spring. As it always will?
Does the chestnut have all time
to candle the earth again? Will Wenzel
and we return? Is this the chestnut rain?

The Ghost

43. (The Binding)

That opening music within the boy and deer, that song
declaring human eyes less beautiful than chestnuts' shining,
those lost children dancing on plastic floors above the loam,
the snow hen's egg candled to a cosmos,
that catalogue lurching among the myriad sources of light, . . .

the tree itself dreamed and tasted in witness time, neighbors
burning plum rot, speaking of peachblow and grapetear,
the ewe's song heard in suburbanite sleep, those deer in stalls,
that train filled with dead who brighten and fade,
the silver-gray steer who cared for flowers,
the foal whose mother may not accept her,
this woman's body tendrilling with semen, . . .

the impure praise for a god of dung and absence,
that railroad tie rotting in an ash wood, soldiers' bodies

passing by way of blossoms into our bloodstreams,
the cross section of chestnut occluded with blight,
churned butter forming on our sight glass,
army rations drying on stoves in mystical autumn
when Li Po's girl picked chestnuts until an auction
when we first see and touch those leaves of a dead girl's gift,
that heartwood tunnel into which the dreamtrain turns, . . .

Wenzel during the gathered moments at rest,
or resisting another world, or winking his clotted socket,
or calling grackles and blackbirds with his chestnut whistle,
Mrs. Wenzel preparing scrapple,
that long section haunted by what our farmers knew,
the simple sacrament of wool harvest,
the ram's butchering, the dream of the lamb's two hearts —

all these, and the others, and those still to come —
drawn together, in ordered time,
arrivals over the years, not one unwelcome,
not one not able to disappear
into the wild carrot's central black star,
but sewn together, bound in doeskin,
boxed in chestnut as strong as the rain.

44.   (Diary Entry: Nocturne)

1.

A fall ago, in rain,
I planted a three-foot Colorado
blue spruce,
unballed it from burlap
into a hole of mud I dug
outside my window.
The tree has taken,
has pushed brown caps from new growth.
As I enter this,
the tree breathes
starlight, as it will when
I am dead.

2.

Here, in my new eyes,
this is its first spring. How easily
it shed the snow that buried it! Already,
a pair of song sparrows nests
within its complex darkness —
blue needles
so sharp that no snake or owl
could climb or strike through.

3.

Maybe without seeing them —
except for knots
of chestnut feathers
at breast centers, they are plain,
streaked sparrow-browns —
you've heard their song, three
short, spaced notes
all at the same pitch, then
jumbles of trills in quick
pitch changes,
but the basic theme, begun
with three notes.

4.

The parent sparrows watched from an ash.
I could just see in:
their eggs were greenish white,
speckled and blotched in shades
of bark-reds and -browns.
Now, I am nearer, and
nearer dead.
What color is starlight under
the four nestlings' lids?
How, and from where,
does that other color
enter their breast feathers?

5.

Evening rain begins again,
seeps into branches where

six song sparrows sleep. Listen:
I am speaking from the center
of the power holding all
together:
my voice remembers
the nestlings' cheepings,
the parents' full songs, their
three spaced notes,
the ascendent, descending trills
into the night, nocturne gathering
rain and breathing blue tree,
touching the nestlings'
breast feathers
and the listening dead, and you, with
chestnut blood.

45. (The Spruce in Winter)

     Because the spruce is a creature of blue light,
because it lives here in winter dusk
     as though to welcome slowly descending darkness,
   because two sparrows sang three notes until
I listened,

     from this hour I again ordain myself,
if I am the blood of blue sound into syllables,
     the one who hears spring sap hum in the holy tree,
   who tastes spruce blueness on the black air.
Be with me.

46. (Two Stories)

I have spread out in front of me again,
leaves of a tree,
two creased pages of newsprint.
For some reason, I have their two stories by heart.
Tell me, my friend, why I have kept them,
what their inner-rhythms are,
and how to speak of them,

of George Schwartz who, in 1907, just a boy,
listened to a Union veteran sad
not to have saved anything,
not a cap or boot-heel or blue rag
or bit of shrapnel to remember Manassas by,
to help him know, with a piece of the solid world,
that he was there, and had not dreamed it.

Schwartz became historian
of the 309th Artillery in WWI,
for sixty years kept everything he could
of his brave, beloved men
who dug gun-pits and graves in French soil in 1918.
Long after, men in their eighties came to him, he said,
to smell belt- or holster-leather,

to touch fingers to faces they once were.
When I close my eyes,
I see him standing young in French air in sunlight
that would turn to dust
behind the 309th's crossed-cannon emblem
unless he and his men remembered.
Now they are all dead. As dead as

Captain Henry Waskow from Belton, Texas,
a small town north of Austin,
who was brought down lashed to a mule
in the next war, off the rainy mountain
at Migano, Italy, in moonlight. The 36th Infantry,
shoulder patch a big "T" looking like a cross
mounted on an arrowhead pointing downward,

lost 8,000, killed or missing, by 1945.
A correspondent stood in the trail
when Waskow's mule was led down,
its burden balanced across a wooden pack saddle,
Waskow's helmetless head hanging on the left side,
his stiff legs sticking out on the right.
"This one was Captain Waskow," a soldier said,

as a group of men pressed closer to say goodbye.
One straightened the points of the captain's collar,
rearranged the torn uniform around the wound,
and walked away. Waskow was twenty-four,
would probably have become a teacher,
his sister said, and married, and had children.
It seems that Henry died before he lived, she said.

Two creased pages of newsprint,
two stories, leaves of a tree
whose roots reach deep as any heart
into loam and chest, into history.
Schwartz and Waskow,
part of that army once described
by Tacitus in all its glory,

the legion's iron-tipped lances, shields,
helmets, breastplates, chariots
gleaming in the Roman sun,
invincible, resplendent, its general
overlooking all and . . . weeping, because, he said,
in a hundred years
these men would all be dead.

47.   (American Time)

When I heard the old woman speak
of a hilltop tree remembered
from her Illinois girlhood —
a bur-oak with top-heavy
lobed leaves and deep acorn cups,
maybe spared by or too big already for a farmer
working prairie into pasture
a hundred years before her —
when I heard her wonder if it lived there still,
when I heard her undersong,

I thought of that tree's limbs arching
the juncture of hill and valley,
girl and country, how the oak's
whole body sang in prairie wind,
buffalo rubbed against its roughness,
men sheltered there one night
and then moved on into the coming strum
of boundary- and trench-wire,
how the tree's cork coat saved it from fire,
how, when the girl climbed it,

she witnessed the changing land's center,
old woman reluctant ever
to travel back there to the tree,

before her womanhood, before the wars, still
wondering whether or not the tree lived,
as it sometimes didn't, but sometimes did,
when she swung her legs again
from a limb of the lone bur oak rooted
above the remembered valley
of American time.

48. (The Communion)

In time, chestnut bark colors rainwater red.
We sip this here in continuing communion.
The war dead enter our bodies in this blood.
The war dead enter our bodies in this blood.

49. (The Trophy)

The deer's head is auctioned off for a few dollars,
  lifted by sunlit antlers to a bidder in the back row.

He's so old, ten-pointed buck who once fed on mast
  in the chestnut hills and valleys of this county,

his brown neck and forehead fur have gone gray,
  moths have notched his ears that heard

wind speak through leaves and branches where he lay
  as the night awoke with what were godly eyes to him

  before he slept, dreamless, or, if this is the way things are,
dreamed of passing above this congregation, saw himself

  not as he was that day in the chestnut wood before he died,
but bodiless, like this, as I am,

  something other-than-himself but still himself, ghost
over this same land, as human noise goes on, the deer

  carried within this nimbus, the last bone
and fur vestige of that being he still is.

50. (The Masters)

Despite the masters, their musics once welcome
but now hysteria's undersong, I dream
that gate open one last time to paradisiacal fields
where Wenzel's sheep graze until world's end,

which could be near. But steady, this story is already
almost told. Paranoid sheep
push their noses into our palms. This last time,
there are dog packs here, not just us

as we sometimes are, but we'll protect the flock,
for lilacs are in bloom, it's spring,
the animals remember nothing of seasons when
we smeared nostrils with tar against bore-worms,

sprayed poison into ears to kill maggots.
Today, it's necessary just to stand in Wenzel's fields
as his metal sheep surround us. That farmer, in fact,
still sleeps, as never before, this late. Today,

we won't make him work the plucking drum,
or keep him busy quartering lambs. Not this time:
in fact, he may be dead, so no matter that the masters
stream over the black meadows of his farm —

they'll leave us alone if we huddle on the median
between lanes, but couldn't care less if they killed us,
the masters, their musics once welcome
but now hysteria's undersong.

51. (Conclusion: The Song)

We have been borne from sleep in a train —
        fields filled its windows,
    ponds of blue-black light, deer and bear

                in the dark distances of dream,
        dirt roads shadowed
            with goldenrod and lilac,

        prairies edged with twilight horizon fire,
tract houses cloned
            against nervescape cities,

valleys of trees gray in the mists of morning.

    Our rails are tarnished silver
                but could bear us
     from the past to somewhere we'll remember
when we near it —

        if we can hear that song (if
            we can hear that song)

within the chestnut rain. . . .

52. (Epilogue: The Ghost)

*A stunted chestnut rises out of the roots of an old stump to tell a stark and
mournful tale. . . . The chestnut was possibly the most loved and useful tree in
America. It was everywhere in the Eastern forest, a towering giant. Its lumber was
strait-grained and durable, suited for many uses, while its nuts were a delicacy to
squirrels, bears, wild turkeys, and the patrons of the well-known figure of his day,
the vendor of roasted chestnuts. Then the mysterious chestnut blight, a fungus,
arrived without warning from Asia. It was first discovered in New York in 1904,
but spread rapidly, causing a forest disaster far greater than either white-pine
blister rust or Dutch elm blight. In the Southern mountains the chestnut was
almost totally eliminated by the early thirties. Now these gaunt and ghostly fellows
strain to survive, but the blight has already claimed them.*

                                        — Michael Frome
                            Whose Woods These Are (1962)

Ahead,
shadowed,
a dead chestnut rears up its trunk, opening eyes where limbs
   have fallen, other limbs still there
as the tree strains up.
He steps,
he begins to get the pale form's shape:
arms chilled by wind and rain, the chance permanence of the
   rain's breastbands, the silvery drapery of the snail
   around the stiffened knees, the knees scarred:
a scarf down the long bole, a streak of veil, of
   shroud.
He lifts his camera. He puts his eyes to the vertical viewer
   and adjusts for light, for distance. His finger presses
and he has it,
the live American ghost.

                                          — Millen Brand
                                      Local Lives (1975)

*The fungus was a visitor native to Japan and China that, like so many intro-
duced pests, found better pickings away from home, and few or no natural checks.
In this case, the immigrant swept the field in less than half a century. Old roots
still send up suckers . . . but so far they are only ghosts.*

— Millard C. Davis
The Near Woods (1974)

As this was growing,
the chestnut bur sent me by a friend split open.
One pearl, but natural, the tree's perfect seed, floated inside.

For a few minutes, I wet the pale nut in my mouth —
it tasted like the smell of grass clogged under your mower,
the smell of old barns —

then potted it in loam,
watered it most weeks for two years,
gave up on it,

but a seedling broke surface,
unfolded. It is still so small,
little ghost, it cannot cast a shadow,

even its seed leaves are lobed smooth.
The storied teeth will have to bite
through soft gum to make their own edge.

Ten hours a day, a plant light shines down on it.
I want to care for it as though,
if it lived, I could climb it to an afterlife,

and you with me. Modern books tell me we
and it and heaven are already dead, but last night,
believe me, when the light above it was out,

when I walked by on my way to sleep,
the seedling spoke one word, or *was* that word
without saying it. The clay pot I'd placed it in

shone like a silver chalice, the chestnut's
several leaves were gauze white
in light from nowhere. I stood there

wanting to hear that word again,
that bead of white tree-sperm on my tongue,
white of all colors, ghost light. . . .

Later, when I fell asleep deeper than I'd ever been, I —
no, I've told enough of mine, you
have that dream,

or my seedling will never flower that needs another
if its ever going to shower
white blossom.

~ from ~

Brockport, New York: Beginning with "And"

(1988)

Dandelions

And this twisting wire

into my cabin in the trees, beneath this acre, below
lion's teeth, air white with them again. . . .

A snowy owl's nest, pellets of mice bones. . . .

In the nursing home, sprays of widows' white
and gray-blue hair. . . .

Driving in fog above the city, I see my parents' ghosts. . . .

Death's-head Himmler wears a white-gold snake ring,
but it's all only spring dandelions,

seed-puff time. . . .

Dresden Gals Won't You Come Out Tonight

This evening I saw scraps of paper floating
like candles on black water,
and thought of you, Li Po,
who lived a thousand years ago,

but these are melodies of a hundred
thousand melancholy poems floated
uselessly in your name along the American river,
so goodby, friend, I

won't mention you again, your language
a silly dream to me,
the same one you had: home,
wine, poetry, plum blossoms,

and the moon.
Vaporized blood. Shadow bone.

Wildflower

1.

Each early summer on this acre,
a single Jack-in-the-pulpit
in woodshade.

If you've ever seen one, its vertical spadix
arched over by its purple-
streaked cowl,

you know the beauty of wildflower.

2.

We walked from my cabin past the flower already
past its bloom, only its bent black stem
left to return

to the world of shades. I didn't show him:
between episodes of delirium tremens,
he was already a dead man —

I knew I'd never see him again.

3.

Believe: the next day, miles away in wine country, an auctioneer
held up this small, iridescent, amethyst,
Jack-in-the-pulpit bud vase.

He called it poetry in black glass. I lowered my eyes,
but bid for it, and bought it. Its hood
leans over emptiness always

to hold wildflower.

(John Logan, 1923-1987)

Winter Letter to Dave Smith

1.

I've been reading your essays on Warren, and last night,
as his "bright-frozen red-bead of a blood-drop" shone,

I dreamed us lost in a future storm, under Virginia pines:
it's dusk, we are seventy or eighty, we hear the war's

grapeshot and chainsaw undersong. I'm wounded,
dragging my left leg along. I cup my palm

on your neck. You're blind, your pupils drops of blood,
but their red laser-light sweeps rays

in the blowing snow and blackness. You say we will live
through everything. I believe, and guide us by your words.

2.

Outside my Brockport window, high-bush mulberry
still hold translucent blood-drops above snow.

When thaw reaches here, the first male redwings
up from your south will have them. The berries

shone here before Seneca women ground them, before scars
formed fierce John Brown who drove his sheep hard

along the Erie Canal towpath a block away —
American dream, we of our generation

who write it, that necessary wildness Emerson
assigned the poet, your blood-drop eyes.

Brockport, New York: Beginning with "And"

And it is Friday, and August,
and now traffic subsides
and the haze of roadside dust
disappears. Our lawn
darkens into evening.
A daddylonglegs ascends a dandelion stem
in effortless eyelash meters that anyone
would want to speak,
and tiny firefly lanterns wink against
our red maples' blood-red black-red bodies.
The air, as air still will, cools
and sweetens.

Our lives here in this port town
vanish, but slowly, but vanish.

Would it help to scream? Would it help to leave?
Some neighbors' children have grown up,
some of the children's parents have died,
always to remain for them
in series of still, and fond, and boring poses
that will never alter, no matter
their children's ages or even should winds
savage as flames sweep our streets.

If it is true, as Li Po prayed it might be,
that ourselves and our shadows and the moon
will meet again in the Milky Way,
his "Cloudy River of the Sky,"
if it is true,
and if it is true . . .

And toward the Thruway, in the shopping centers,
package stores glow in lights the colors
of their own liquors, drugstores
in aspirin-white fluorescence. Now
lines at the bank
thin out, a ton of paychecks
cashed and ready for sorting. And.
And couples in the corners of the bars whisper
maybe sex, maybe cancer, maybe
the end of another summer.

We are looking out over evening
where the years begin. We talk,
saying the same things:
five Augusts more, or one, or forty,
now or later, we and/or/and
our friends will die, our children travel
to their own ends,
but someone, if we awaken into the old prayer,

as billions of grassblades lose their light,
as maples rise sable-red within the black air,
as years number us further and further away,
as stars course their patterns
and earth flows Li Po's eternal river,
someone will know, and remember,
and be set dreaming,
and will say "and."

If You Know Me at All

I once prayed that this acre be the elm's home,
but my elms are dying, or dead. Today I dragged
almost the last torso to the back line
for mouse- and rabbit-shelter over the long winter.

Babe Ruth, whose decorum on formal occasions I sometimes
for the health of my soul have needed to emulate,
said near his end that termites had gotten into him,
and as I hauled elm bats away across autumn,

my right elbow and left knee ground out their lamentation.
But I am used to them by now, and almost
unafraid. Me and the Babe and the elms got
a season or so to go before we're nothing here

but sawdust. I root for them, as you will,
with me, if you know me at all. In elm bark we see
children on diamonds over which the sun passes,
and all our home runs in the cross-cut growth rings.

Milkweed

One acre, for now, to hold to. Entrusted
(these days that thought is almost dead).
Most is wooded — ash, maple, some small elm
which live, for now, but may be last of their kind
despite my prayer that this acre be the elm's home.

There's one corner I've wanted to clear
to plant giant sunflowers there —
I picture them in their meditation
bending their necks above my head, gold-
petaled eyes seeing everything before

autumn pecks them blind — but milkweed took over:
I can plant sunflowers somewhere else, and will,
but still the unborn souls of those
not planted in the milkweed corner
come toward me, some knee-, some genital-, some

heart-, some brain-high. . . . But the milkweed
now deepen into green;

later, their stems will flutter
orange and umber monarchs
that lay their eggs only on them. . . .

What are, where are the children I didn't have,
anyway? . . . Maybe biding in time where all
the disincarnate dwell, while I walk earth
in their places, doing what I can
to sense, love, and name them.

Memorial Day, Brockport, 1981

We stand under cemetery maples.
The high school band has played Keyes' questioning anthem.
Seven veterans stand at parade rest, the oldest
from WWI, the youngest from Vietnam.

A minister prays aloud for the dead,
for those who survived, for peace for us all.
I close my eyes, inhale scents of flowers on the graves,
drift in remembering shadows through the day. . . .

A wavery trumpet remembers "Taps." The vets fire blanks.
Our village shivers in the sound.
Then, a minute's silence while an undecided sky
goes on with sun and clouds

as though for this, for something here
impossible to say, as soldiers raise our flag again.
God bless these living soldiers, and the dead. Sometimes,
we needed them. Now we live with what they've done.

Brockport Sunflowers

If they could walk, they would walk slowly.
They would shuffle onto our roads from their fields,
lally-gag into our village, sway on sidewalks,
dangle their silly and beautiful heads.
Sexless, they would not bow to women,
or shake men's hands with their leaves.
Desiring nothing but sunshine and water,

they'd peer into our shops with amazement.
Seeing themselves in windows, they'd know themselves holy.
They would love the children, and listen to them,
all day long, until the children were ready for bed.
As the evening star rose in the heavens,
they would nod goodby to us, not having said a word,
and return, like walking haloes, to their fields.

Blackberries

Once more, before their patch disappeared
under the last months of winter,
I walked across glazed snowcrust to see them.
Teeth had gnawed the cane tips, etched
white-on-white ice micetracks ringed them.

My western mind's middle eye, trying
not to notice nothing, noticed a scatter
of rabbit pellets, an insect's egg-
sac impaled on one thorn, even chlorophyll dots
on the single remaining leaf among the canes.

Then, somehow, nothing. No
body in its boots. Emptiness. White time
or white lightning flash. . . . Then, again,
the canes. I knelt to pick this
mysterious gift, blackberries.

Arrows

        That year spring snowmelt
    and rain had risen
into my cabin —
        for days I dredged silt,

        rock, and leaf-muck
    from the run-off ditch, built
a bank that felt
        right. My arms ached, my back

warned me to stop.
   I knelt, a last time, to pick
up a half-stuck cedar stick.
      Its flat tip

      seemed notched,
   rounded sharp.
At its end, a shape
       emerged from washed clod

      clumped on this bluer-
   than-cedar wood, and glinted:
a quartz arrowhead.
      I knelt there

      as I kneel now, again,
   in time, the one interior river
bearing me, that hunter,
      you, and my frail cabin

      back like dreams into the deer's eye,
   the hawk's breast, the last chamber
of wolf- or bear-heart where
      all our arrows rot, and fly.

The Berries

My wife already there to comfort,
I walked over icy roads
to our neighbor who had lost her father.
The hard winter starlight glittered, my breath
formed ascending souls that disappeared,
as he had, the eighty-year-old man
who died of cancer.

In my left coat pocket, a jar
of raspberry jam. . . . I remembered
stepping into drooping canes, the ripe
raspberry odor. I remember bending over,
or kneeling, to get down under leaves
to hidden clusters. . . .

Then, and on my walk, and now, the summer berries
made/make a redness in my mind. The jar
presses light against my hip, weight
to hand to the grieving woman. This gift
to her, to me — being able to bear
summer's berry light like that, like this,
over the ice . . .

When I was a boy, the Lord I talked to
knew me. Where is He now? I seem to have
lost Him, except for something
in that winter air, something insisting on being
there, and here — that summer's berries, that mind's
light against my hip, myself kneeling again
under the raspberry canes.

The Geese

At my desk at school grading compositions in late September —
distant notes of Canada geese waver through my screens,
those melodious signals up and down their lines.

One student, a Seneca, writes of her father in the woods,
keeping him company alive and now for ten years
after her one central terror.

The geese keep calling from high above our village,
calling to her.
Her father levels his rifle. To see him, she half

closes her eyes, the way all writing must begin:
gray and black geese in the shimmering autumn sky, a father
desperate to kill even an out-of-season doe, and gunfire.

The Beam

This autumn evening,
I point my flashlight behind my cabin
to sunflowers where I know they are.

I watched them grow all summer,
but never looked for them in darkness.
I didn't know they were this lonely,

drawing me toward them along the beam.
Nothing else inhuman in my life
has known me before as they do,

this family bending above me,
halos around their heads. If my friend
were here with me again,

he'd talk to them to tell them,
in their own ancient language,
how some of us believe them. Each year,

among their slim, leaf-draped bodies,
I'll try to hear his voice, wherever he's gone,
already. Soon, as he did,

the sunflowers will drop their heads
all the way down. This evening,
intimate but earthbound, only half true,

but true, the beam focuses here.
That loneliness I blamed on them
was only mine, for now, for him.

                                        John C. Gardner (1935-1982)

~ from ~

Falling from Heaven

(1991)

The Dead

A survivor, years later, allowed himself to wonder
where the dead were,
all those hanged from beams in their own barns,

or slaughtered against walls,

or herded to their own orchards, shot into ditches,
or starved in cattlecars to camps,
who screamed for God in the agony showers,

who burned their ways into graves in the empty sky. . . .

But then, at last, he saw one, one thin woman in a cloud
in a blue dress wisping away from her,
dress he'd bought her fifty years before.

"There you are," he said,

"there," and "there," as others appeared from the west
in bursts of sunlight and cloud,
whole families of them, streets and villages of them,

cities of them, clothed in vapor, returned

by rails of sunlight, by sweeps of cloud, in carriages
of burnished cloud.
He kept waving, kept crying out,

"Here, here I am, *here,*"

but as for them, they sailed over his head, horizon
to horizon, for the rest of his life,
doing all they possibly could — forming, eddying,

obeying the wind.

Coin

What was a Jewish child worth, summer, 1944,
when the Nazis halved the dosage of *Zyklon B*
from 12 boxes to 6 boxes for each gassing?

When released, the gas rose, forcing the victims
in their death struggles to fight upward,
but the gas filled every pocket of air, at last.

What was a Jewish child worth when the Nazis,
to save money, doubled the agony
by halving the gas? 5 marks per kilogram,

5.5 kilograms invested in every Auschwitz chamberload
of 1500 units. With the mark at 25¢
this meant $6.75 per 1500 units,

or 45/100 of a cent per person. Still,
this was too much: sometimes the rationed gas
ran out during the long queue of consumers,

so children were thrown alive into the furnaces.
In the summer of 1944 at Auschwitz, a Jewish child
was not worth 1/2¢ to the Reich

which struck this coin, floating freely hellward now
into that economy, this twenty-five-mark piece,
one risked mark for each line, gas

for more than sixty children for each line,
if it please God and/or the Nazis in their mercy
to at least gas them before they are heaved

into the flames of the Thousand Year Reich.

The Candle

It would do me no good to travel to Auschwitz.
It would do the dead no good, nor anyone else any good.
It would do me no good to kneel there,
me nor anyone else alive or dead any good, any good at all.

I've heard that in one oven a votive candle
whispers its flame. When I close my eyes,
I can see and feel that candle, its pitch aura,
its tongues of pitch luminescence licking the oven's recesses.

A survivor, forty years later, crawled up into an oven and lay down.
What of his heart? Could it keep pumping its own pitch light
here where God's human darkness grew darkest?
Whoever you were, please grant me dispensation.

Rudolf Hess praised the efficiency of these ovens.
It would do me no good to travel to Auschwitz, to kneel or lie down.

It would do me or God or anyone else alive or dead,
or anyone else neither alive nor dead no good, no good at all.

The survivor did crawl back out of the oven.
He took his heart with him, didn't he not, it kept beating.
He left his heart in the oven, and it keeps beating, black-black,
black-black, the candle of the camps.

Eyes closed, staring up into this, eyebeams of pitch luminescence,
and the pulse of it, the heart, the candle — you and I,
haven't we not, have met him, the one who lay himself down there
where the Nazis had missed some, welcome, welcome home. . . .

We have spoken the candle heart of the camps.
It does the dead no good, nor us any good, doesn't it not,
but it keeps, black-black, its watch of pitch light,
and will. Any good at all. Wouldn't we not? The candle.

The Apple

(for Elie Wiesel)

I

In Israel at that time just after the war,
we did not have much to eat,
so when, at the beach, I saw an apple bobbing in the waves,
glistening red, far out, but an apple for sure,
I swam for it.

I did reach the object,
and, as I'd thought, it was an apple.
I carried it to shore in my bosom,
thinking of its juice and firm flesh.
But, inside, it was rotten:

it had been thrown from a boat,
or a cloud, for good reason.
Were you to eat a bit of my survivor's heart
even the size of an apple seed,
it would poison you.

II

In Israel at that time just after the war,
we did not have much to eat,

so when, at the beach, I saw an apple bobbing in the waves,
glistening red, far out, but an apple for sure,
I swam for it.

I did reach the object,
but it was not an apple.
Unbelievable as this might be, it was an eye,
perhaps from an octopus, or a shark,
or a whale, but an eye,

translucid red, a watery gel,
its pupil black and unmistakable.
Perhaps this was the eye of the angel
of the camps. I cupped it in my hands.
I swallowed at least one mouthful, to see.

The Secret

The survivor spoke. I began to hear.
Not her cattlecar four eternal days from Budapest,
the dead buried under luggage in one corner —
I'd heard this before.
Not the shorning, the aberrant showers, the corpse stink of soup —
I'd heard this before.
Not the electrified barbed wire —
but as though her sentences
shorted themselves out,
phrases that buzzed & crackled
under her breastbone barracks. Not music,
the gaunt band playing the walking dead off to slave labor,
back from slave labor —
I'd heard this before, or tried to. But
red streaks of voice across
an ionized atmosphere,
gassed Hungarian clawhair & ribnails & tongues, a burst heart
breaking into static as she spoke,
into cancelling sparks,
her now never-ending speechlessness, never.

~ from ~

Pterodactyl Rose

(1991)

Harpoon

                   Now that blue whales are as few as two hundred,
          I want the last one dead.
I need to forget them right away,
          before the last reports:
                   ships stripping lost codes of flesh,

                   the last calf wandering away, &, later,
          are there any left?
Before the last eye is cut out, dumped overboard,
          & floats away,
                   & what it sees. Kill them now, please,

                   before politics can't save them —
          the fountaining overtures
the biblical jaws the blue tinge fathoms deep
          the evolutionary curves our
                   predecessors' pitiful & beautiful last songs.

Dodo

Large. Flightless. No predators.
Secure on Mauritius ten million years.
Slow moving. Trusting. Ungainly
and beautiful. Eyes gray, maybe —
no one knows for sure.

Dutch sailors. Later, colonists'
clubs and dogs. The last
dodo died in 1680. Ungainly
and beautiful. Eyes pink, maybe —
no one knows for sure.

Ate the fruit of *Calvaria major,*
the dodo tree, which could not propa-
gate itself without its dodo, ungainly
and beautiful. Eyes blue, maybe —
no one knows for sure.

By 1970, only thirteen trees, the last
of their species in this world, were left. . . .
The dodo sometimes seemed to smile, ungainly
and beautiful. Eyes black, maybe —
no one knows for sure.

To germinate, the tree's seeds
needed to be crushed
in the dodo's craw. Ungainly
and beautiful. Eyes ochre, maybe —
no one knows for sure.

On other secret intricacies, it's mum,
and will be. In the British Museum,
I saw one stuffed one: ungainly
and beautiful, one socket
empty, one sewn shut.

Stuff

In the duplication center I xerox a hundred pages
of the usual stuff, you know the stuff.
I xerox maybe a branch's worth, maybe

a small lower branch of Georgia loblolly pine:
evergreen scent of toner, & when I close my eyes,
I see the long needles of light along my branch.

Sometimes, the stuff done, it takes a touch
from next-in-line to break the spell
of xerox, fire, & the wheel.

Gods of Vanished Species

At Kwik-Fill, I pump ferns and turtles into my tank.
They'll ride here in my dark until they burn.
Millions of years later, now, our traffic
traverses ancient landscapes, zone by zone,

desert by forest by marsh by swamp until
we sleep. At night, like you, I almost remember
rib-like sprays of cattails, pterodactyl eyes of coal,
clouds of insects curving a moonlit shore.

Pterodactyl Rose

Like you I drive my ten
thousand American miles a year
burning fossil fuels (conversion
to a ton or two of carbon)

but maybe unlike you I peer
into my rear-view mirror imagining air
filling with insects & plants maybe
Triassic dinosaurs

turtles Devonian dragonflies & lilies
such beak & leaf & wing & vine
profusion the past assuming
extinction's shape behind me where I'm going

wild with this prayer of mine,
& longing.

The Real News

When I bought *The Real News* because a human skeleton
had been photographed on the moon,
when I stared at bones in tatters of rags,
the skull leering sidewise into a landscape of craters
on that arid cell of cosmos,

I knew I'd been born a sucker, and, in any case,
over that world and its imagined time,
whatever time it was, our earth still shone, didn't it, familiar
continents in outline where teeming billions still
breathed trees and pure water.

Fast Food

I sit at McDonald's eating my fragment of forest.
The snail and slug taste good, the leaves,
the hint of termite and bat, the butterfly trans-

substantiated by steer karma, and mine.
Another pleasure: to breathe distillate of foam
scented with coffee and chemical cream.

Another virtue: groups of us all trained
the same way, millions across America
where we flourish, at present, under the golden arches.

The Gift

Because, he said, he didn't want,
because he didn't want them,
because he didn't want them to live,
because he didn't want them to live in poverty,

rainforest Governor Amazonino Mendes distributed
two thousand free chainsaws
to his peasant constituents because
he didn't want them to live in poverty,

& it's easy, it's easy for me,
it's easy for me to start this, easy
for me to fill my own chainsaw with gasoline & oil, easy
for me to start this chainsaw snarling, to say

that with his gift Mendes cuts off the feet
of the peasants' children, clearcuts
the family trees of his constituents, easy
for me to speak with a chainsaw tongue

as the trees fall, as the air burns & darkens,
as the forest's blanched soils wash into gullies
because I want peasants to live under trees,
because I want them to live in poverty,

because money means that my nearby mall
carries the perfect gift, & I can easily afford it:
a teak desk set, box inside a box, envelopes,
paper, knife, & a whole roll of U.S. stamps.

A Jar

Each noon, at the construction site around the corner
from my own wooded suburban acre,
I checked progress: the bigger trees — almost all ash,
a few maple, one white oak — chainsawed, dragged out
by dozer and chain; then dozer back in for clearing brush;

then dozer, backhoe, and ten-ton roller to cut
foundation-, drainage-, and sewer-pipe patterns
into subsoil and clay, to pack dirt so it would never shift.
Day by day, in drizzle or shower, hot sun
or one sudden out-of-season jet stream shift to chill,

the men widened the site's geometric margins
to where, in one corner, piles of trucked-in sand
diminished a twenty-foot puddle filled for weeks
with thousands of tadpoles just beginning
to grow legs and lose their tails. The time would come,

of course, to fill this last swale. Meanwhile,
the polliwog population prospered in this lukewarm
algae-sweetened pond of their world. . . .
And then was gone, all at once, their birthplace leveled
with sand and a few inches of good topsoil

over which we walked. That was that, except
for this, the one thing, the thing in itself:
how, at about this time, our species began to document
amphibians' disappearance across the globe;
how marshes and swamps were growing silent;

and how, an actor in our sentimental elegy, one worker
placed in his tool chest to take home at quitting time
a jar filled with muddy water and a host of tadpoles,
little blips of sperm-shaped black light.
To catch them, he must have knelt and cupped them in his palms.

The Swamp

Stretched out underwater, neck telescoped forward,
smelling the spring mud as though just waking,
behemoth walked in a drowse. Braced myself,

hauled it in two pulls by its fat tail to shore
where it blinked and shut itself off to such nonsense,
withdrew its neck to wait out whatever. . . .

Noticed a leech necklace, glints of topaz in its eyes,
nostrils protruding upward so it could breathe while
hidden in muck with its jaw open,

its pretty pink inviting tongue wiggling.
Fed it a stick: it struck in a hiss and snapped it.
Thought of creatures it had eaten —

even an adult blue heron piteously broken,
leg by wing, at last dragged down in mid-cry.
Wanted to end this snapper and all its children

in their primitive armor, wanted to boil it,
eat its heart, digest it at leisure in a trance of bliss
in my own top-of-the-food-chain arrogance, . . .

but if we rid the world of snappers, would mosquitos cloud
when herons ate all frogs? Was there balance here,
or have we come too far filling in wetlands, forcing

every last heron into the snapper's jaws? Yearned
to knife its voracious brain to the ground,
but wanted to do the precarious right thing, you understand. . . .

In the end, wouldn't act alone. Looped a wire
around its shell, tied it to a tree with enough play
so it could just reach water or climb ashore. . . .

We've all summer to decide. If you want me to,
I'll ax its ugly bejeweled head off, or let it loose.
Listen to the swamp, and let me know.

Matrix

When I was a boy,
I found a mutilated turtle
emerging from mud.
Something, when it was young,
had broken its shell
almost in half,
but the shell,
as though welded with glossy solder,
had mended;
something had chewed
its back legs to the joints,
but its stumps were hard.
How did you survive,
I asked it,
but it was mute, still half adream

from its winter sleep.
I spoke to it,
warmed it in my boy's hands,
but it boxed itself up. . . .

For some time
after her mastectomy,
weeks of hospital and chemotherapy,
my wife woke toward me
in slow spirals,
as though from ether,
unsure of where we were
or how we'd live
in our new matrix
of scar and fear.
But it was April, again.
In windows before us,
as we changed her dressings,
the days rained, and warmed.
One morning, I pressed my lips
to her chest until, at last,
she believed,
and opened up to me,
our answers so slow to come
that came.

Crickets

Evenings, where lawns are not sprayed with poisons,
you can still hear the crickets,
you can still see lightning bugs signaling,

look, a yellowgreen strobe under the trees,
but gone, but there again, sometimes
in the same spot, and sometimes not,

as the tiny purveyors of phosphor
drift past our houses, looking
for one another, and the crickets,

crickets, crickets, the ones that still
have their legs, keep scraping them together,
listen, maybe for the last time on earth, listen. . . .

WILLIAM HEYEN

William Heyen was born in 1940 in Brooklyn, New York. His undergraduate degree is from SUNY at Brockport, where he is now Professor of English and Poet in Residence; his graduate degrees are from Ohio University. A former Senior Fulbright Lecturer in American Literature to Germany, he has been awarded two fellowships from the National Endowment for the Arts, a John Simon Guggenheim Fellowship, the Eunice Tietjens Memorial Prize from *Poetry* magazine, and the Witter Bynner Prize for Poetry from the American Academy and Institute of Arts and Letters. His writing has appeared in many periodicals including *American Poetry Review*, *Harper's*, *TriQuarterly*, *Ontario Review*, *The New Yorker*, *The Southern Review*, and in more than a hundred anthologies. For *The Host: Selected Poems 1965-1990*, William Heyen has chosen poems from eleven previous collections.

Also available from **Time Being Books**®

LOUIS DANIEL BRODSKY
You Can't Go Back, Exactly
The Thorough Earth
Four and Twenty Blackbirds Soaring
Mississippi Vistas: Volume One of *A Mississippi Trilogy*
Falling from Heaven: Holocaust Poems of a Jew and a Gentile
  (with William Heyen)
Forever, for Now: Poems for a Later Love
Mistress Mississippi: Volume Three of *A Mississippi Trilogy*
A Gleam in the Eye: Poems for a First Baby
Gestapo Crows: Holocaust Poems
The Capital Café: Poems of Redneck, U.S.A.

HARRY JAMES CARGAS, Editor
Telling the Tale: A Tribute to Elie Wiesel on the Occasion of His 65th
  Birthday — Essays, Reflections, and Poems

ROBERT HAMBLIN
From the Ground Up: Poems of One Southerner's Passage to Adulthood

WILLIAM HEYEN
Falling from Heaven: Holocaust Poems of a Jew and a Gentile
  (with Louis Daniel Brodsky)
Erika: Poems of the Holocaust
Pterodactyl Rose: Poems of Ecology
Ribbons: The Gulf War — A Poem

TED HIRSCHFIELD
German Requiem: Poems of the War and the Atonement of a Third
  Reich Child

VIRGINIA V. JAMES HLAVSA
Waking October Leaves: Reanimations by a Small-Town Girl

RODGER KAMENETZ
The Missing Jew: New and Selected Poems

NORBERT KRAPF
Somewhere in Southern Indiana: Poems of Midwestern Origins

ADRIAN C. LOUIS
Blood Thirsty Savages

JOSEPH MEREDITH
Hunter's Moon: Poems from Boyhood to Manhood

FOR OUR FREE CATALOG OR TO ORDER

(800) 331-6605
Monday through Friday, 8 a.m. to 4 p.m. Central time
FAX: (314) 432-7939